For Grades

EXPERIMENTING

with ART

25 EASY-TO-TEACH LESSONS IN DESIGN AND COLOR

By Shirley Kay Wolfersperger and Eloise Carlston

GoodYearBooks

An Imprint of ScottForesman
A Division of HarperCollinsPublishers

Dedication

This book is dedicated to our children:
P. J., Barrett, Jennifer, and Jean Marie.

Good Year Books are available for preschool through grade 6 and
for every basic curriculum subject plus many enrichment areas.
For more Good Year Books, contact your local bookseller or
educational dealer. For a complete catalog with information about
other Good Year Books, please write:

Good Year Books
Scott, Foresman and Company
1900 East Lake Avenue
Glenview, IL 60025

Preface

Experimenting with Art is a book for teachers and parents who are not professional artists or art instructors. It is a how-to book in the strictest sense: it contains information on how to teach design and color fundamentals to children. Though the book is designed for third through sixth grade, first- and second-graders are capable of completing the experiments in small-group instruction. Even older children and adults who have not yet had this sort of instruction can benefit from the experience of this book.

The objective of the book is to help students gain a working knowledge and understanding of how an artist uses design and color concepts to create a work of art. By studying the concepts, completing the experiments, and doing as many enrichments as possible, students will gain the basic tools necessary to help them create works of art of their own and appreciate the art of others.

Very often art instruction is passed over and ignored in the elementary grades. It is precisely in these grades that a good basis should be taught. All children are artists, and they have a wonderful sense of good design. This book tries to enhance that. It contains twenty-five lessons that build from the very simple to the more complex concepts. Your students will benefit if you present the concepts in order.

Each lesson introduces and discusses a main idea or concept. Then the children do several art "Experiments," which reinforce the concept and help the students explore its possibilities. The experiments are generally very simple to do and most are illustrated in the lessons. Each lesson has one or more worksheets that you may copy to reduce the preparation time of the experiments. The final "Lesson 25: Unity Worksheet" may be used as a pre-test, as a review study sheet, or as an end-of-course assessment.

The directions for the "Experiments" and "Enrichments" are for you, the teacher. You may want either to read the directions to the class or to explain the directions to the students in your own words. Doing the experiments and enrichments yourself beforehand is a good idea, but not altogether necessary in every case.

The classroom time for explaining and illustrating each lesson's "Concept to Be Taught" is approximately twenty minutes. The additional time for the experiments varies. You may teach one lesson in a class period or during several periods.

The "Enrichments" follow the experiments. These projects are more complex than the experiments and also help illustrate and reinforce the "Concept to Be Taught." The students will profit from as many enrichments as time allows.

At the end of the book, there is an "Art Source" that correlates famous paintings to the concepts taught in each lesson. Prints of these famous works are generally available in public or school libraries. You can illustrate and further explain the lessons by showing the students all or some of these reproductions.

As you will see, this course needs no elaborate setup. The experiments usually can be done with the simplest of materials—white paper, construction paper, black marking pens, crayons, colored markers, etc. The enrichments often need more varied supplies, but they are fun to do and are very thought-provoking.

We strongly suggest that you urge the children to work in the abstract as often as possible. By using the term "working in the abstract," we mean that the children should draw using no recognizable objects. We all have had students who seem stuck in ruts of heart shapes, houses, or sharks. In order to get the children to experience as much of good design as possible, it is necessary that they break away from old habits.

We also recommend that you mount the students' designs for display. In developing this curriculum, we have found that exhibiting the drawings as often as possible works as powerful positive reinforcement.

As you teach these lessons, remember that the great thing about art is that there is no "right" or "wrong." There are no definitive answers for the experiments. The basic elements and principles of design and color are not ironclad rules, but only suggestions for how to make a design more pleasing.

Table of Contents

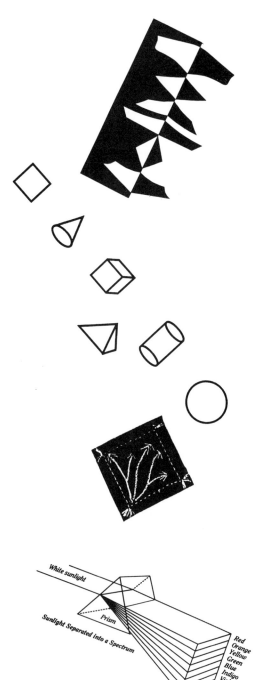

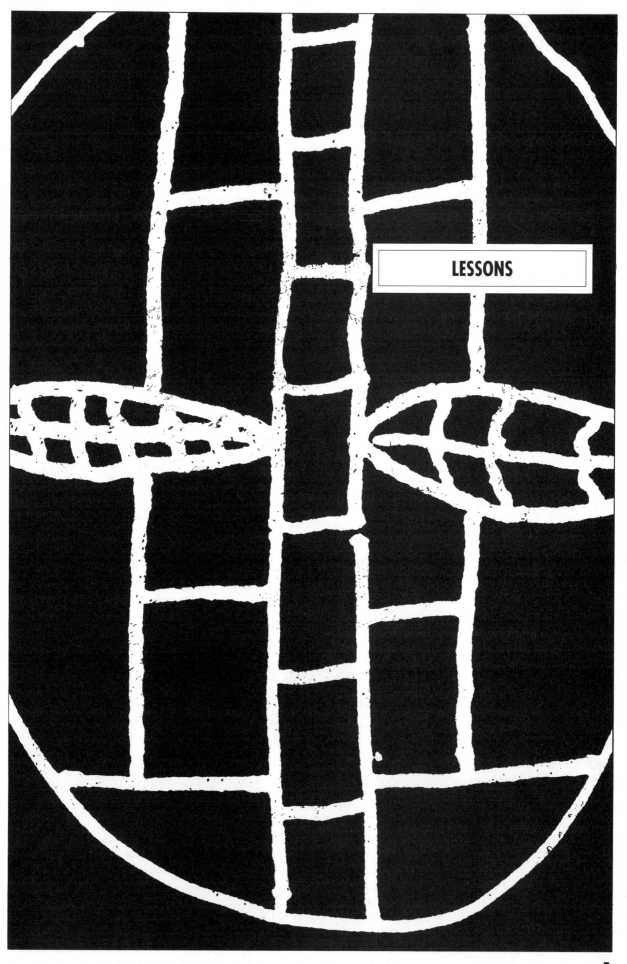

LESSONS

CONCEPT TO BE TAUGHT:

There are several building blocks in basic design. The first one is a "point." A point is simply a dot. A single point has power. The more points there are, the less power each point has. For example, one dark speck on a large white carpet catches our attention. We look at the dark speck first before we really see the whole carpet. But if there are many specks on the carpet, they would not grab our attention in the same way.

Using several points, we can make a design. This type of art is called "pointillism." Pointillism is a school of painting that uses paint in small points or dots to create a picture. Georges Seurat, who lived in France during the late 1800s, was a famous pointillist. Today, points are used in printing newspaper and comic book pictures, and television uses thousands of points to create the picture on the screen.

MATERIALS:

White drawing paper, black markers (or black crayons), colored markers (or crayons)

EXPERIMENT **1.** View newspaper and comic book pictures with a magnifying glass.

EXPERIMENT **2.** With a black marker on a half sheet of white paper, make an abstract design using points.

EXPERIMENT **3.** Draw a picture entirely of points using colored markers on a half sheet of white paper.

EXPERIMENT **4.** Use the Points Worksheet *(page 53)*. Or using a black marker, draw at least twenty-five random points. Connect the points with lines to make interesting shapes.

ENRICHMENT:

Colored Points: *Glue dots punched from colored paper onto a black background to make a design.*

Pinpoint Patterns: *Using colored construction paper, cut out interesting shapes. With a pencil, lightly draw a design on the shape. Next, with push pins or straight pins, punch holes closely along the lines. Hang the shapes by strings in windows so that light may be seen through the pinpoints.*

From Experimenting with Art *published by Good Year Books. Copyright ©1992 Shirley Kay Wolfersperger and Eloise Carlston.*

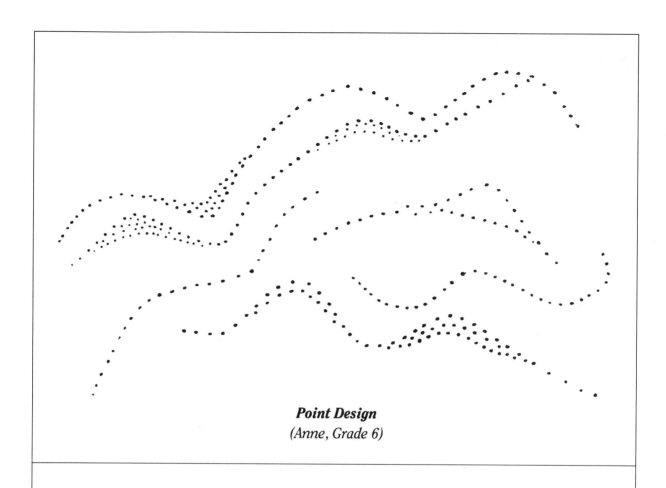

Point Design
(Anne, Grade 6)

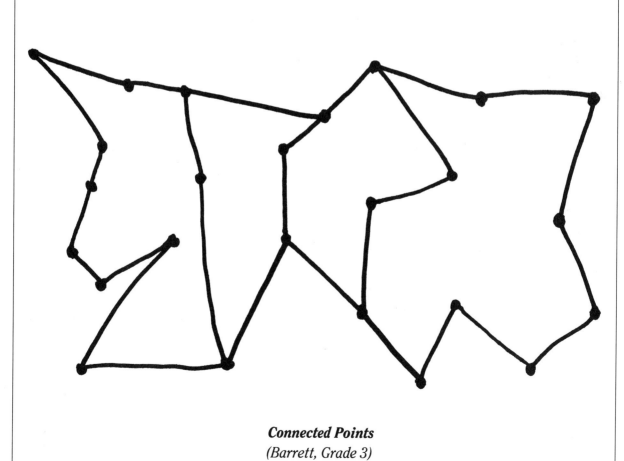

Connected Points
(Barrett, Grade 3)

CONCEPT TO BE TAUGHT:

A line is a mark that has a beginning and an end. Lines can be made with almost anything: pencils, crayons, and chalk obviously make lines, but string can also make a line. Edges of objects are lines as well. Lines can be straight, curvy, bumpy, jagged, or wavy. They are very important to an artist. Lines can tell us what the artist is trying to communicate through his or her art. We can show moods and feelings, such as anger, laziness, confusion, or happiness, by drawing different kinds of lines. These are called "character lines."

MATERIALS:

White drawing paper, colored markers (or crayons)

EXPERIMENT 1. Examine the classroom to find examples of lines and edges that form lines. Discuss.

EXPERIMENT 2. Use the Lines Worksheet *(page 54).* Or on white paper folded in fourths, draw character lines with markers and label them ANGRY, LAZY, CONFUSED, and HAPPY.

EXPERIMENT 3. On a half sheet of white paper, make a design with markers using lines only.

ENRICHMENT:

Blow Painting: *Place a blob of watercolor paint on white construction paper. With a straw, blow at the paint to form lines. Continue with other colors until an interesting "blow painting" has been made.*

Outline Design: *On a large sheet of white paper, draw four or five interesting shapes. Use two, three, or four different colored markers. Leaving a little space each time, begin repeating the outline of the shapes until they connect and fill the page.*

From Experimenting with Art *published by Good Year Books. Copyright ©1992 Shirley Kay Wolfersperger and Eloise Carlston.*

Angry

Lazy

Confused

Happy

Sample Lines

kristen

Line Design
(Kristen, Grade 1)

CONCEPT TO BE TAUGHT:

Lines can be used to show motion by guiding and moving our eyes around a design. Horizontal lines guide our eyes across the paper. They create a calm and restful mood in a design. Vertical lines move our eyes up and down the paper. They make us think of buildings and trees. Diagonal lines move our eyes from one corner of an object or design to the opposite corner. They are exciting lines and show strong feelings.

So that our eyes don't leave the design, we must stop the motion with shapes or other lines. For instance, a roof stops the up and down motion of the walls of a house, and a flower stops the direction of its stem.

MATERIALS:

White drawing paper, colored markers (or crayons)

*EXPERIMENT **1.*** Use the Direction Lines Worksheet *(page 55)*. Or with markers, draw stop-motion lines on white paper folded in thirds. Label them HORIZONTAL, VERTICAL, and DIAGONAL. Remember to stop the motion of each of these lines with another line or shape.

*EXPERIMENT **2.*** Using markers on white drawing paper, make a design using stop-motion lines. Use curving, zigzag, and bumpy lines or shapes to stop the motion of other curving, zigzag, and bumpy lines.

ENRICHMENT:

Paper Weaving: *Fold a sheet of construction paper in the center. Starting at the fold, cut straight or curvy lines of different widths. Using one or two contrasting colors of construction paper, cut strips of varying widths. Weave these strips through the cuts of the first paper. When the design is finished, trim and glue the loose ends. Both sides of the design are equally interesting.*

Variation: Cut out and glue on small pieces of colored paper to decorate the strips after they are woven.

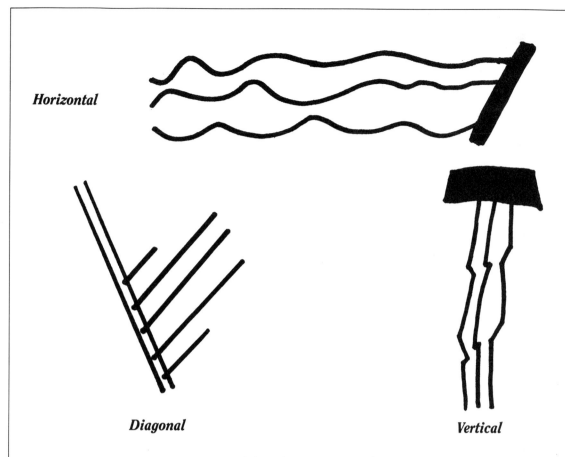

Horizontal

Diagonal

Vertical

Direction Line Samples

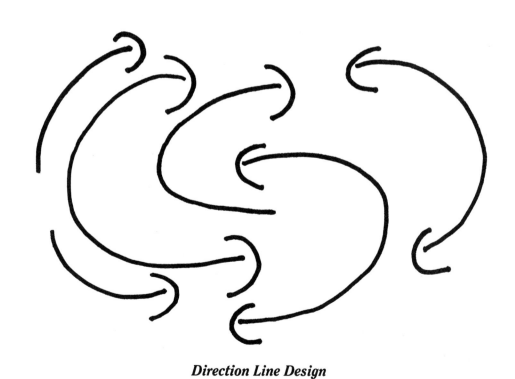

Direction Line Design
(Anne, Grade 6)

CONCEPT TO BE TAUGHT:

When both ends of a line meet to surround space, the line forms a shape. Shapes can be familiar, such as squares, triangles, or circles. They can be made from curvy or straight lines. Shapes can have bumpy or pointed edges as well. They can be things we don't recognize, or they can be things that we do recognize, like an octopus or a snowflake.

Point, line, and shape are related like families are related. A line goes between two points, and lines become shapes that form designs.

MATERIALS:

White drawing paper, black construction paper, colored and black markers (or crayons), rubber cement (or paste)

EXPERIMENT **1.** Use the Shape Worksheet #1 *(page 56)*. Or fold white paper in half. Using markers, draw and label SHAPES WE RECOGNIZE on one half of the paper. Include circles, triangles, stars, etc. On the other half, draw and label SHAPES WE DON'T RECOGNIZE. Include curvy, bumpy, and pointed shapes.

EXPERIMENT **2.** Use the Shape Worksheet #2 *(page 57)*. Or with black construction paper, cut out *five* rounded shapes, like stones, of different sizes. Place them in an interesting pattern on white paper. Glue them down. Imagine the stones are in a stream or waterfall. Using black markers, draw lines on the paper, showing how water would flow around the stones. Mount the design on black construction paper.

ENRICHMENT:

Waxed Paper Transparencies: *Put down two layers of newspaper with a large piece of waxed paper on top. Cut tissue paper of several colors into interesting shapes, and arrange the shapes on the sheet of waxed paper. Add cut pieces of yarn to make interesting lines. Carefully place a sheet of waxed paper over the design. Then put more newspaper on top and iron with a medium-hot iron to bond the waxed paper together. Cut off excess waxed paper and hang designs in windows.*

Fabric Shapes: *Cut interesting shapes from different pieces of fabric. Glue the shapes onto colored construction paper. Outline the shapes with yarn using liquid white glue.*

From Experimenting with Art *published by Good Year Books. Copyright ©1992 Shirley Kay Wolfersperger and Eloise Carlston.*

Shapes We Recognize
(Meghan, Grade 2)

Shapes We Don't Recognize
(Adam, Grade 3)

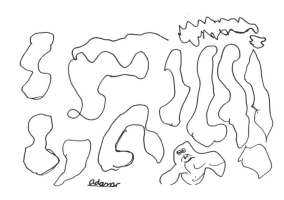

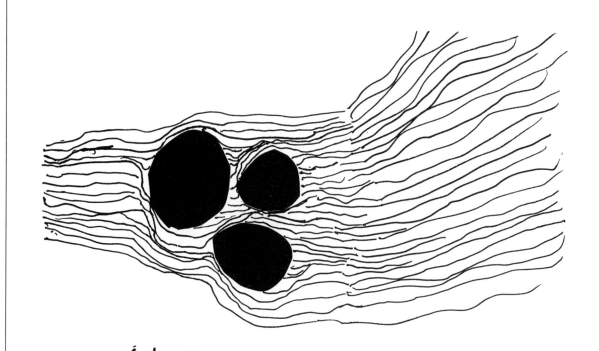

Rock Problem
(Adam, Grade 3)

CONCEPT TO BE TAUGHT:

A contour is the outline of an object. The contour of a ball is simply a circle, and the contour of a quarter-moon is a crescent. Drawing contour lines of any object or living thing is good training for the eyes and hands of beginning art students.

There are many different ways to practice contour drawing, and the results can be unexpected. For experiments 2 through 6 below, use a different object for the subject of each drawing. Do not be concerned if the drawings do not look real or are distorted. While drawing, remember not to lift the pencil from the paper. If there is time, do more than one "contour" drawing for each experiment.

MATERIALS:

Magazine pictures, 8 1/2" x 11" sheets of newsprint or scratch paper, pencils, colored markers, objects for drawings, such as: cup or mug, tea kettle, pineapple, ukulele or guitar, hat, vase with flower, student model, stack of books

EXPERIMENT 1. Use the Contour Worksheet *(page 58)*. Or cut pictures from magazines and use markers to outline the contours.

EXPERIMENT 2. Draw the outline of an object while looking at it the entire time. Do not look down at the drawing.

EXPERIMENT 3. Draw the outline of an object using the hand normally not used for drawing.

EXPERIMENT 4. Draw the outline of an object, making the drawing upside-down while looking at it right-side up.

EXPERIMENT 5. Study an object for two minutes. Remove it from sight, and draw the outline of the object from memory.

EXPERIMENT 6. Study an object for two minutes. Close your eyes and draw the outline of the object.

ENRICHMENT:

Still Life: *Arrange several interesting objects on a table. Draw an outline of the entire arrangement without lifting the pencil from the paper.*

From Experimenting with Art *published by Good Year Books. Copyright ©1992 Shirley Kay Wolfersperger and Eloise Carlston.*

Drawing While Looking

Drawing with Other Hand

Drawing Upside Down

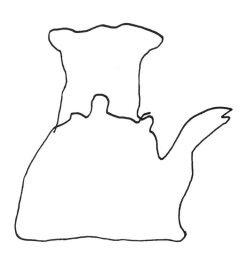

Drawing from Memory

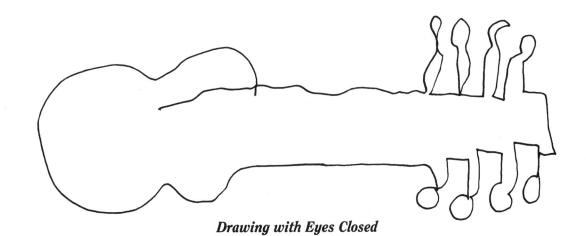

Drawing with Eyes Closed
(All Drawings: Anne, Grade 6)

CONCEPT TO BE TAUGHT:

A form is a shape that has three dimensions: height, width, and depth. A flat shape has only two dimensions: height and width. Form represents the difference between drawing a square on paper and drawing a cube. A form always has bulk or mass.

Some basic forms are the sphere, cube, cone, cylinder, and pyramid. Shapes from nature or man-made objects are variations of these forms. For instance, a pine tree is a cone, and a building is a cube. More complex subjects are combinations of these basic forms, such as the human body. It is made of various cylinders and a sphere.

MATERIALS:

Magazines, scissors, tape, tracing paper, pencils or black markers, white drawing paper

EXPERIMENT **1.** Use the Form Worksheet *(page 59)*. Or draw and label the basic forms: CONE, PYRAMID, CUBE, CYLINDER, SPHERE.

EXPERIMENT **2.** Cut out a magazine picture. Tape a piece of tracing paper over it. Using a pencil or black marker, outline the basic forms in the picture.

EXPERIMENT **3.** Darken the classroom. Shine a flashlight on various objects to emphasize the forms. Discuss and relate the objects in the classroom to the basic forms.

ENRICHMENT:

Clay Creatures: *With modeling clay, make all five basic forms. Put the basic forms together and smooth out the edges to create an alien creature. Add details made from additional clay.*

Polyhedra: *Research and draw other three-dimensional shapes, such as a tetrahedron, hexahedron, and a dodecahedron.*

Soap Sculptures: *Show various sculptures, feeling and viewing each one from many angles. While looking at a large bar of Ivory soap, imagine a fruit, a fish, or some other object emerging. Begin carving slowly, using a paring knife and scraping carefully. When sculptures are completed, smooth with a wet finger, and paint with water colors. Spray with clear fixative.*

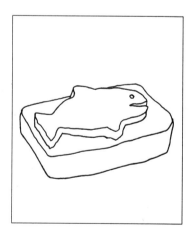

*The human shape is made of various forms: the head is a sphere, and the
trunk, legs, arms, fingers, and toes are cylinders.*

(From Traditional Japanese Design Motifs *by Joseph D'Addetta. New York: Dover Publications, 1984)*

CONCEPT TO BE TAUGHT:

Size refers to how big or how small something appears. Size in a drawing is decided by comparing one object to other objects. For example, in a drawing with two horses standing next to one another, it is easy to see which is larger. In a drawing with one horse, it is hard to tell much about its size.

An artist can use size to show distance on flat paper. A horse that is drawn smaller on one piece of paper will appear farther away than one that is drawn larger on another piece of paper.

When an artist draws a flower larger than its normal size, the flower is more important because of its scale. Scale is used by an artist to show exact size differences between objects. Scale also helps us make a large drawing into a small one, or a small drawing into a large one.

MATERIALS:

White drawing paper, pencils, colored markers (or crayons)

EXPERIMENT **1.** Starting on one side of a sheet of paper, draw a large shape with a marker. Repeat the same shape many times, drawing it smaller each time.

EXPERIMENT **2.** Use the Size Worksheet #1 *(page 60)*. Or with a pencil make a picture that fills a sheet of paper. Draw the same picture as accurately as possible on a quarter sheet.

EXPERIMENT **3.** Do the Size Worksheet #2 *(page 61)* on "squared enlargements."

ENRICHMENT:

Treasure Maps: *Create island treasure maps. Use small drawings to represent different locations on the maps, such as caves, rivers, and volcanoes. Then mark Xs to show the way to the treasure. Maps may be colored, coated with salad oil, and have torn edges to look like parchment.*

Comic Enlargements: *Cut out a comic square from a magazine. Draw a pencil grid over the comic using one- inch squares. Make another grid on larger paper using two-inch squares. Make sure there are exactly the same number of squares on each grid. Now, matching squares, "enlarge" the comic.*

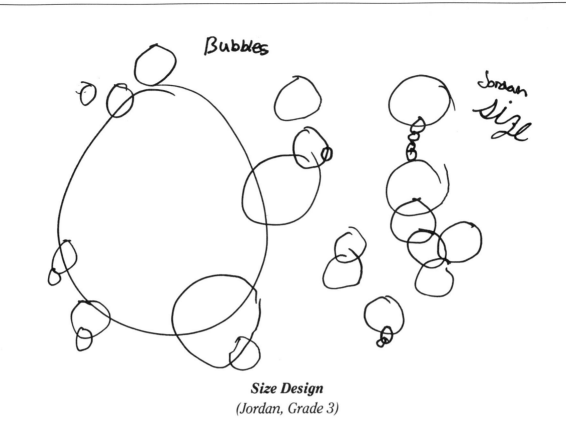

Size Design

(Jordan, Grade 3)

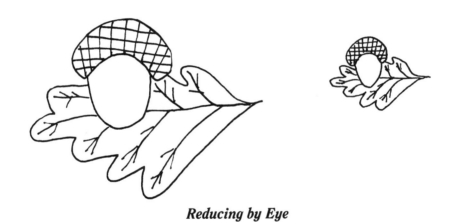

Reducing by Eye

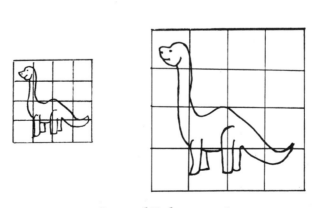

Squared Enlargement

From Experimenting with Art *published by Good Year Books. Copyright ©1992 Shirley Kay Wolfersperger and Eloise Carlston.*

CONCEPT TO BE TAUGHT:

Texture refers to how the surface of something looks and feels. For example, the surface of a brick is hard and rough. A snake's skin is scaly and dry. An artist can represent texture through points, lines, and shapes: points can show the scratchy surface of sandpaper; long, flowing lines can show hair; and small circular shapes can show the dimples on a golf ball. The shapes forming a texture can create a pattern, such as a brick wall or a shingled roof.

MATERIALS:

White drawing paper, pencils, dark crayons

EXPERIMENT **1.** Examine all the objects in the classroom, noting their textures and how they might be represented by points, lines, and shapes. If desired, bring additional textures from home to form a class collection.

EXPERIMENT **2.** With paper and a dark crayon, do texture rubbings of classroom items. Share the rubbings with the class. View them with a magnifying glass to observe details, if desired.

EXPERIMENT **3.** Use the Texture Worksheet *(page 62)*. Or fold a piece of paper into eight sections. Label each section with one of the following: BRICK, GRASS, WOOD, FUR, SANDPAPER, HAIR, GRAVEL, and CLOTH. With pencils, draw a texture in each section.

ENRICHMENT:

Relief Rubbings: *Do rubbings of coins, embossed book titles, greeting cards, ceramic tiles, rough lumber, burlap or other highly textured fabrics. Use the side of a soft-leaded pencil, crayon, or colored chalk.*

Fish Printing: *Obtain a fish with head, scales, fins, and tail. Place the fish on newspaper and dry it with paper towels. Brush the fish lightly with black ink and place a piece of paper over it, pressing gently. Pull the paper off carefully to reveal the textures.*

Book Rubbing
(Jean, Grade 4)

Brick	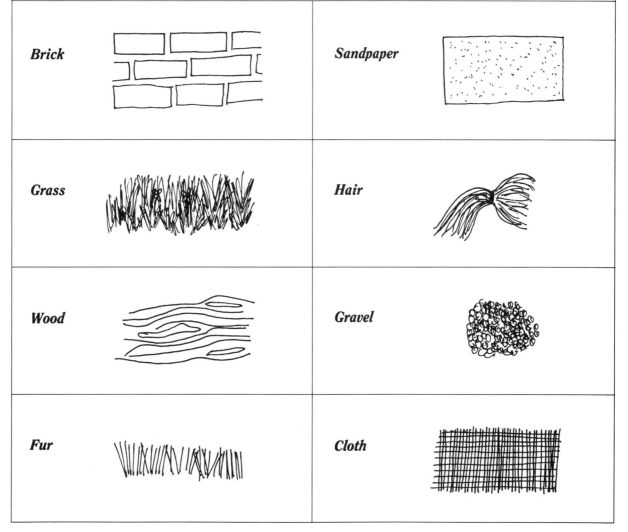	*Sandpaper*	
Grass		*Hair*	
Wood		*Gravel*	
Fur		*Cloth*	

CONCEPT TO BE TAUGHT:

Repetition and rhythm are the repeating of parts within a design, such as shapes, colors, or lines. Repetition involves using similar things over and over again, while rhythm refers to using them in an order or pattern.

Repetition and rhythm are just as important to art as they are to music. The rhythm is the beat, and the repetition is the chorus sung again and again. In music, our ears pick out the rhythm. In art, our eyes pick out the pattern in a drawing and follow it.

MATERIALS:

White drawing paper, colored markers (or crayons), rubber bands (or paper clips, strips of paper, etc.)

EXPERIMENT 1. With markers on white paper, create a design in which *nothing* is repeated.

EXPERIMENT 2. Use the Repetition Worksheet *(page 63)*. Or with markers on white paper, create a design using a shape that is repeated, such as a circle, triangle, or rectangle. You may add lines and points as well. Compare the first experiment with this one.

EXPERIMENT 3. Arrange ten to fifteen rubber bands into patterns on paper. It is not necessary to glue them down. View all of the designs by walking around the room.

ENRICHMENT:

Patterned Wallpaper: *Look at samples of wallpaper. Design a patterned wallpaper for your bedroom with markers, crayons, and colored pencils.*

Potato Printing: *Cut large potatoes in half. With a pencil point, draw an interesting, but simple, shape or pattern on the cut face. Cut away the parts that should not be printed. Apply poster paint lightly to the potato with a brush. Print onto paper by pressing the potato down firmly and evenly. You may wish to make wrapping paper or other patterned art.*

Non-Repeating Design
(Chris, Grade 2)

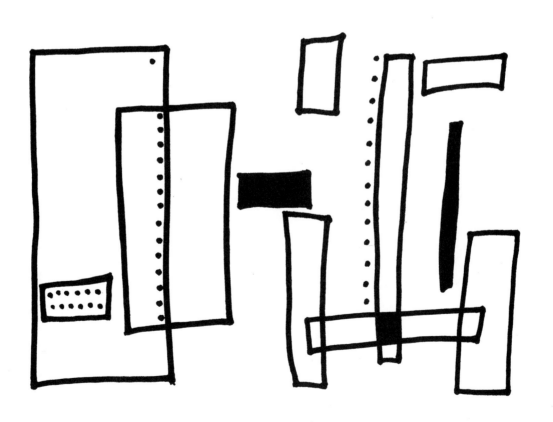

Repetition Design
(Michael, Grade 5)

CONCEPT TO BE TAUGHT:

In order for a design to be interesting, it must have contrast and variety. Contrast refers to having different things in the same design, such as in a design of circles, where the contrast might be a half circle. In art, the opposite of contrast and variety is repetition and rhythm. Repetition helps make things in a composition the same, but too much repetition is monotonous and boring, so contrast helps make things different. Each is needed for a perfectly balanced design. The eye likes to see certain elements repeated, yet also wants to see the differences.

MATERIALS:

White drawing paper, colored markers (or crayons)

EXPERIMENT 1. Use the Contrast Worksheet *(page 64)*. Or using markers and white paper folded in fourths, make and label contrast drawings of each of the following: TALL & SHORT, CIRCLE & HALF-CIRCLE, SMOOTH & JAGGED, and LIGHT & DARK.

EXPERIMENT 2. Using markers and white paper, draw a design with a shape that can be repeated. Add whatever contrast or variation that seems pleasing.

ENRICHMENT:

Wooden Spoon Animals: *Give each student three small, flat wooden spoons or cut-out cardboard shapes of wooden spoons. Glue the shapes on paper in an interesting arrangement. With black markers, outline the shapes and add details to make different animals. Color with crayons or markers.*

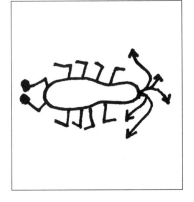

Ice Cream Sodas: *On brown paper sacks, use a pencil to draw the shape of a large soda glass overflowing with ice cream. Plan contrasting layers to fill the glass using points, lines, shapes, and textures. Paint with poster paints, making sure that one color is dry before adding another. Cut out the ice cream sodas.*

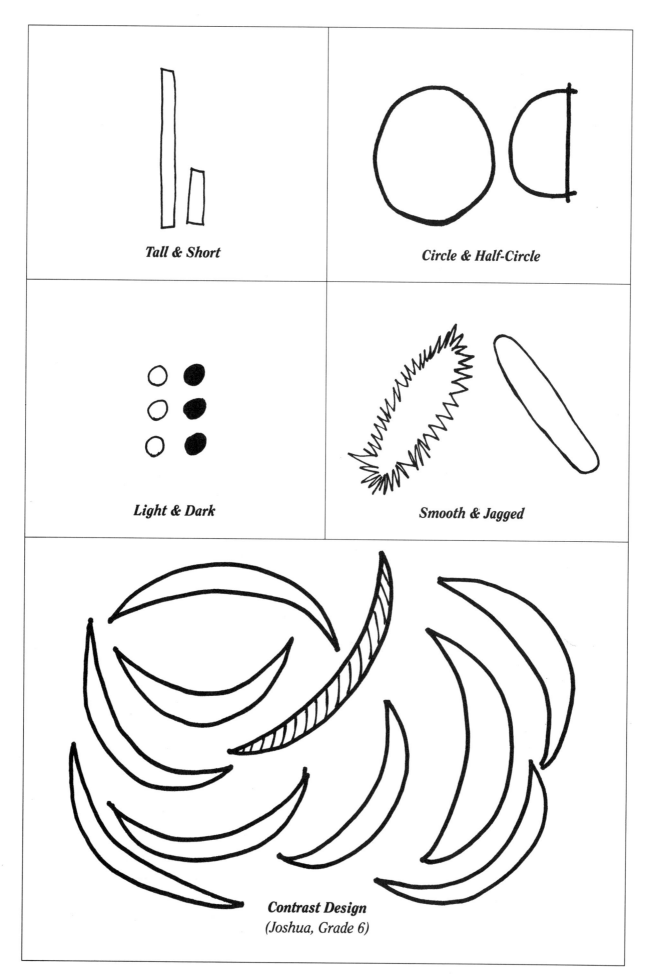

Tall & Short

Circle & Half-Circle

Light & Dark

Smooth & Jagged

Contrast Design
(Joshua, Grade 6)

CONCEPT TO BE TAUGHT:

Dominance refers to making one part of a design or picture more important than the rest. All other details are less important than the dominant part, but they also add to the drawing. An artist can make something stand out by its size, color, texture, shape, position, or any combination of these. For instance, in a drawing of black shapes that are the same size, a smaller red shape would be dominant. Or a single triangle can be dominant over a group of triangles if it is away from the group. Artists often, but not always, make the center of a picture the dominant area. The focal point, the place where the eye keeps returning, usually is in the dominant area. All drawings should have some kind of dominance.

MATERIALS:

White drawing paper, colored markers (or crayons)

EXPERIMENT **1.** Use the Dominance Worksheet *(page 65)*. Or using markers and white paper folded in quarters, make miniature drawings showing dominance and label them: SIZE, COLOR, TEXTURE, and SHAPE.

EXPERIMENT **2.** With white paper and markers, draw a human eye that fills the page. Make *one* part of it dominant, such as the pupil, the iris, or the eyelashes.

ENRICHMENT:

Tissue Collage: *From several colors of torn tissue paper, make a collage background that covers an entire sheet of white paper. After gluing the tissue down, create a focal point for the collage by cutting out a photograph of a real object from a magazine. Glue the cutout down in an interesting position.*

Pop-Out Masks: *Draw a large mask-type face in the center of white construction paper. With markers, glitter, ribbons, etc., decorate the mask. Next, begin outlining the mask shape over and over again with markers—drawing each outline outside of the previous one—until you reach the edge of the paper. Carefully cut out the mask. If desired, cut out the eyes and discard. Take the outlined background that has been cut away from the mask and glue it onto a larger piece of paper. In the center where the mask was cut out, glue squares of sponge or folded paper tabs. Finally, glue the decorated mask onto the tabs or sponges so that it "pops-out" or stands away from the background.*

Dominance by Size

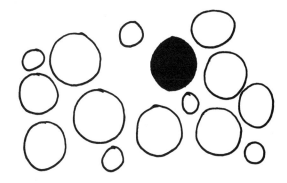

Dominance by Color

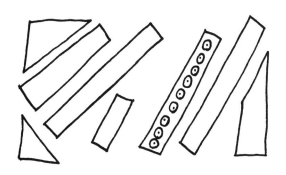

Dominance by Texture

Dominance by Shape

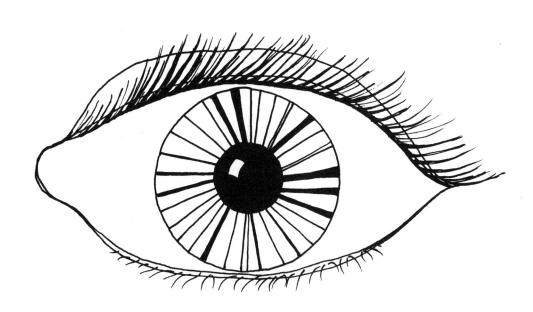

Eye with Pupil Dominant

CONCEPT TO BE TAUGHT:

Balance in a drawing keeps one part of a picture from becoming heavier than another. Balance in art is like a teeter-totter. If there is one child on each end of the teeter-totter and they are both the same weight, the board will balance. But if one child weighs more than the other, the heavier child will have to move closer to the center of the board to make it balance. Similarly, everything in a picture has weight, even the empty space. A line weighs less than a shape. A shape that is filled in with a color or texture weighs more than a shape outline. A form that is three-dimensional weighs more than all of these. Balance in a drawing can be achieved from side to side or from top to bottom. If a design or picture is unbalanced, you as the viewer will feel that something is wrong.

MATERIALS:

White drawing paper, colored markers (or crayons), rubber cement (or paste), colored construction paper

EXPERIMENT 1. Take out items from your desk, such as pencils, pens, erasers, books, etc. Using the desk top as a background shape, put the items in a balanced arrangement. Next, make an unbalanced arrangement. Discuss and compare the results.

EXPERIMENT 2. Use the Balance Worksheet *(page 66).*

EXPERIMENT 3. Cut out seven or more shapes of varying sizes from colored construction paper. Move the shapes around, arranging them on a sheet of paper, until they "feel" balanced. Glue them down.

ENRICHMENT:

Shape Mobiles: *Use colored construction paper to create a mobile of different-sized shapes, such as circles, squares, triangles, hexagons, stars, and crescents. Use long drinking straws and thread to hang the shapes, making sure they balance.*

From Experimenting with Art *published by Good Year Books. Copyright ©1992 Shirley Kay Wolfersperger and Eloise Carlston.*

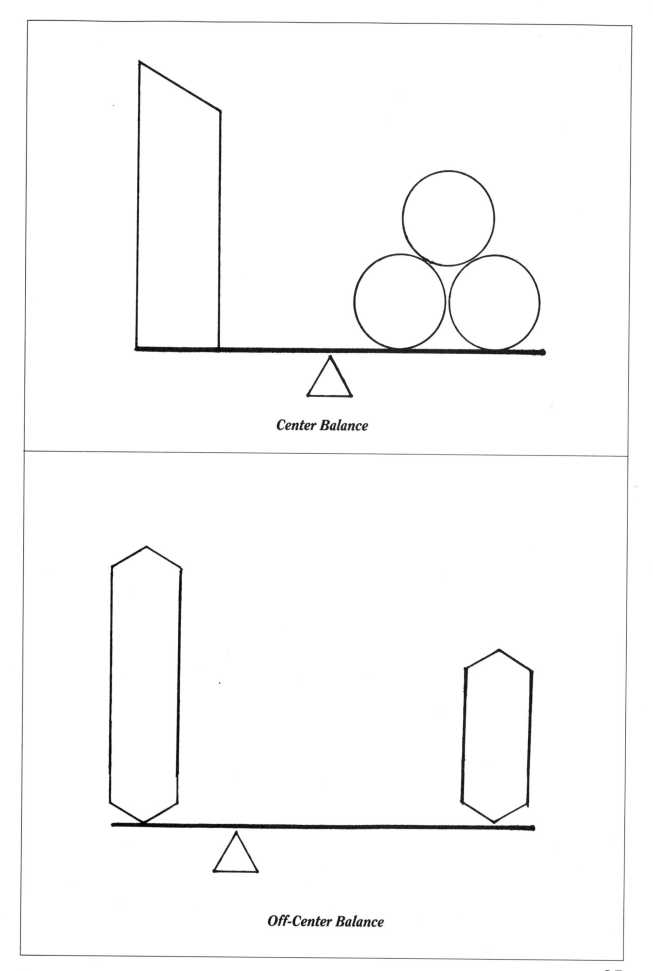

Center Balance

Off-Center Balance

CONCEPT TO BE TAUGHT:

The concept of symmetry, which is related to balance in art, concerns designs that have two identical halves. For example, a butterfly has symmetry, or is symmetrical, because one wing perfectly matches the other. Similarly, the human body is symmetrical because the left half and the right half match.

The butterfly and the human body are examples of what we call "bilateral symmetry," in which one side of an object or design is the mirror image of the other. This is also called "two-sided" symmetry.

Another type of symmetry is "radial symmetry." This type concerns circular designs with a single center, such as a snowflake or a bicycle wheel. Designs that fall into the radial and bilateral symmetrical categories are said to have "formal" balance. Good drawings and designs do not need formal balance, but they do need some kind of balance. (Review Lesson 12 if necessary.)

A drawing that is not the same on both sides is said to be "asymmetrical," and a drawing that is asymmetrical is said to have "informal" balance. Most pictures are asymmetrical and have informal balance.

MATERIALS:

Markers (or crayons), white drawing paper, colored construction paper, scissors, rubber cement (or paste)

EXPERIMENT **1.** Find and discuss examples of bilateral symmetry, such as scissors, windows, people, chairs, and desks. Also discuss and show examples of radial symmetry, such as fruits cut crosswise, flowers, wheels, starfish, etc.

EXPERIMENT **2.** Use the Symmetry Worksheet (page 67). Or after folding a piece of paper in half, use markers to draw and label examples of BILATERAL SYMMETRY on one half and RADIAL SYMMETRY on the other.

EXPERIMENT **3.** Fold a sheet of paper in half. Starting from the fold, cut out an interesting shape, making it as large and intricate as possible. Open at the fold and mount the bilateral shape on colored construction paper.

ENRICHMENT:

String Paintings: Paint an eighteen-inch length of cotton string with different water colors, making sure the string is thoroughly covered with paint. Fold a piece of white construction paper in half. Loop the string in an interesting way on one half of the paper, leaving a short length of string at the bottom for pulling. Fold the other half of the paper over the string and press down firmly while pulling the string out from between the fold.

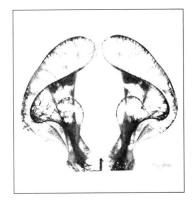

Half & Half Pictures: From magazines, cut out pictures that have bilateral symmetry. Cut these in half, gluing the half-pictures on white paper. Draw and color the missing half.

From Experimenting with Art published by Good Year Books. Copyright ©1992 Shirley Kay Wolfersperger and Eloise Carlston.

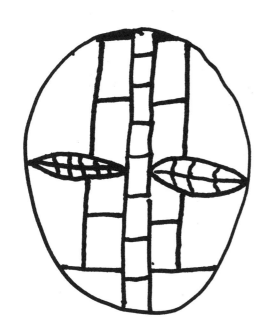

Bilateral Symmetry
(Adam, Grade 3)

Radial Symmetry
(Mandy, Grade 2)

Bilateral Folded Design
(Barrett, Grade 3)

CONCEPT TO BE TAUGHT:

The positive space of a picture is the picture's subject, or what the artist wants us to look at. This space is called the "foreground." For instance, in a picture of an elephant surrounded by jungle, the elephant is the foreground. The jungle background is what we call the "negative space" in the picture.

Negative space is as important as positive space because it surrounds and sets off the positive space. An artist needs to consider both in balancing a design. Without negative space, the positive space loses its power to attract the eye. Even a single point on a blank piece of paper creates positive and negative space and commands our attention.

Artists use "frames" to determine the right amount of negative space surrounding a design. Frames are two L-shaped pieces of paper that you put over a picture and slide back and forth, enlarging and reducing the area around the subject.

MATERIALS:

Colored and black construction paper, white drawing paper, magazine pictures, pencils, rubber cement (or paste)

EXPERIMENT **1.** Use the Positive and Negative Space Worksheet *(page 68)* to construct a pair of frames, or make similar frames from black construction paper. Use the frames over pictures cut from magazines to show various amounts of negative space. Focus the frames on different parts of the pictures to see what changes take place.

EXPERIMENT **2.** Draw a small design on a sheet of paper. Use the frames from the worksheet to determine the right amount of negative space. With a pencil, draw along the inside edge of the frames. Then cut out the picture along the pencil line and mount on colored construction paper.

ENRICHMENT:

Dioramas: *Cut a piece of paper for the background of a shoebox-sized diorama. Draw and color a background scene on it, such as a landscape suitable for dinosaurs, underwater life, etc. Glue the paper around the inside of the box. On the opposite end, cut a small viewing hole. Form clay figures for the foreground and add any other objects desired. Cut a long, one-inch wide slit in the lid for light. View the scene from the "frame" of the peephole.*

Photograms: *Using a light source, place several interesting objects on photosensitive paper, making positive and negative spaces.*

Too Much Negative Space

A Good Amount of Negative Space

(From Treasury of Chinese Design Motifs *by Joseph D'Addetta. New York: Dover Publications, 1981)*

CONCEPT TO BE TAUGHT:

Counterchange refers to switching the background and the foreground of a design, either with colors or with black and white. In other words, we see the design both in negative and positive space. A checkerboard is an example of counterchange. Another example involves a picture of a night sky. The sky is black and the stars are white. The counterchange is a white sky with black stars. Counterchange is not just the repetition of a design; it is the reverse of a design.

MATERIALS:

Colored construction paper, scissors, rubber cement (or paste)

EXPERIMENT **1.** Use the Counterchange Worksheet *(page 69)*. Or choose a sheet of construction paper for a background. Then, with half a sheet of construction paper of another color, carefully cut out a shape. Glue the leftover paper surrounding the shape on one-half of the background paper. Next, take the shape and glue it to the opposite side of the background to form the counterchange.

EXPERIMENT **2.** Use a sheet of construction paper of any color for the background. With another sheet of construction paper that is half the size of the larger piece and a different color, cut out several shapes of different kinds along one edge, and set the shapes aside. Take the leftover piece and glue it down on half of the background paper. Now take the cut-out shapes and place them along the edge, opposite of where they were cut. Glue them down to form the exploded counterchange.

ENRICHMENT:

Counterchange Etchings:

Thoroughly coat a piece of white drawing paper with white chalk. Then place a solid layer of a dark-colored crayon over this. Now, place another sheet of drawing paper over the first one, and draw a design on it using heavy pressure with a ballpoint pen. Separate the papers. The crayoned sheet will be etched with white lines, and the underside of the top sheet will have dark lines. Mount the sheets together to show counterchange.

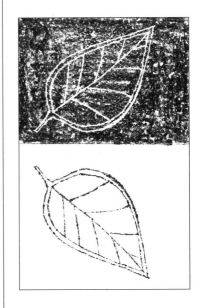

From Experimenting with Art *published by Good Year Books. Copyright ©1992 Shirley Kay Wolfersperger and Eloise Carlston.*

Counterchange Design
(Barrett, Grade 3)

Exploded Counterchange Design
(Jean, Grade 4)

CONCEPT TO BE TAUGHT:

We use the term "value" to refer to how much light and dark is in a design. Value is very important because it makes some parts of a composition more dominant than others. Pure white is the lightest value, and black is the darkest value. All values in between are grays.

Texture and shading are ways of making shapes have value. The more texture or shading a shape has, the darker in value it becomes. For instance, imagine words as texture on a piece of white paper. If the paper has one sentence typed on it, it has a very light value. But the same paper with many sentences typed on it has a much darker value.

Color also has value. A design with a lot of light colors and very few darks is considered a light-valued picture. A design with a lot of dark colors and very little light is considered a dark-valued picture. Most good art is made up of a combination of lights and darks.

MATERIALS:

White drawing paper, pencils, white, gray, and black construction paper, scissors, rubber cement (or paste)

EXPERIMENT 1. Use the Value Worksheet *(page 70)*. Or on white drawing paper with a soft-leaded pencil, make five squares down the page. Using texture or shading, show the values from lightest to darkest. Label them LIGHTEST, MEDIUM-LIGHT, MEDIUM, MEDIUM-DARK, DARKEST.

EXPERIMENT 2. Divide the class into three parts. Have one-third of the class make designs with shapes cut from black construction paper glued on white paper. Have another third make designs with gray paper shapes glued on black paper. And have the final third make designs with gray paper shapes on white paper. Compare the results.

ENRICHMENT:

Fabric Class: *Ask each student to draw himself or herself using a black marker on a piece of white drawing paper. Have them dress the drawings with fabric scraps. One of the fabrics should be a light-valued one and the other a dark-valued fabric. The students should use yarn or colored markers to complete the face, hair, and shoes. With the cut-out figures, make a class bulletin board.*

Black on White Shape Design

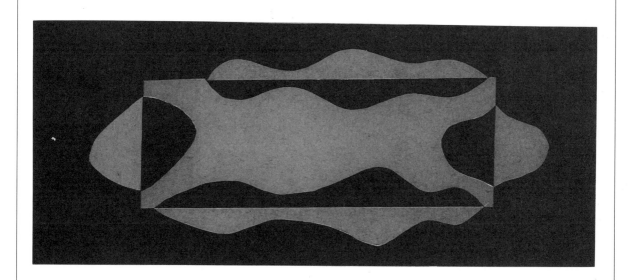

Gray on Black Shape Design

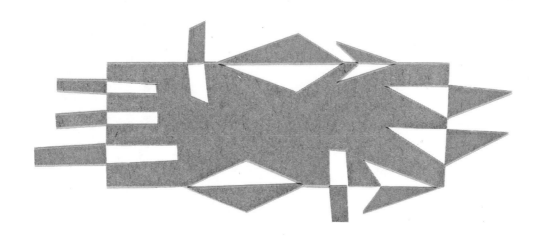

Gray on White Shape Design

CONCEPT TO BE TAUGHT:

Simple perspective is the art of making a flat drawing look like it has distance or depth. One way to do this is to overlap objects, placing one object in front of another. The object that is in front seems to be closer than the object that is behind. Adding a shadow to an object is another way to make it stand away from the paper, giving the object additional depth. A third way to create depth is to draw objects smaller if we want them to seem farther away. For instance, in a drawing of several cactuses standing in the desert, the largest cactus seems to be the closest. The smallest cactus is often higher in the picture and looks farthest away. The drawing of the smaller cactus will also have less detail than the larger one.

MATERIALS:

Construction paper, pencils, scissors, rubber cement (or paste)

EXPERIMENT 1. Cut from construction paper several sizes of triangles, circles, and squares. Arrange the shapes so that they overlap. Glue them down.

EXPERIMENT 2. Go outside on a sunny day to observe and study shadows. Measure the length of the shadows. Also note the direction and shape of the shadows.

EXPERIMENT 3. Use the Simple Perspective Worksheet *(page 71)*. Or draw a desert scene with several cactuses, making the large cactuses near the bottom of the paper and the smaller cactuses higher in the picture to show perspective. You may add detail, shadows, and color if you wish.

ENRICHMENT:

Faux Oils: Draw a picture on cardboard, using the principles of simple perspective. Mix powdered tempera paints with liquid detergent until it looks like thick cream. Paint pictures using short-bristled brushes, table knives, and spatulas building up several layers. Allow the pictures time to dry completely. Spray with a gloss fixative.

Crayon Fireworks: On white drawing paper using crayons or colored markers, make five to seven points in a random pattern. With any color and using short, straight strokes that look like newly cut grass, make a circle around one of the points. Change to another color and make another circle, continuing until there are seven or eight circles around the point. Follow the same procedure with the other points, stopping the colors as they come together, so that the circles look like they overlap each other.

Overlapping Design

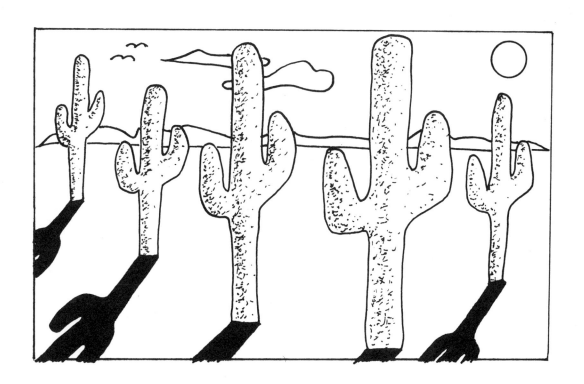

Desert Perspective

CONCEPT TO BE TAUGHT:

Light is made up of different colors that travel to your eye at different speeds. When light travels through a prism, the prism separates the beam of light into its component colors. For example, raindrops can act as prisms and spread a rainbow across the sky.

Because color *is* light, when there is no light, there is no color. That is why colors are so hard to see at night.

A color wheel is a good tool to help teach about the colors that artists use. The wheel puts the colors of the rainbow in a circle and shows how they are related. Color wheels may be simple, with only six colors, or they may have as many as twelve or twenty-four colors. Black and white do not appear on the color wheel, but they are on color spheres, which are very complicated color wheels with hundreds of colors.

MATERIALS:

Prism, white drawing paper, crayons

EXPERIMENT 1. Use a prism to separate sunlight into the colors of the rainbow. Discuss the colors that you see.

EXPERIMENT 2. Use the Color Worksheet *(page 72)*. Or construct a twelve-part color wheel on paper using the worksheet as a model. Color heavily with crayons, starting with yellow at the top. Label the color wheel clockwise: YELLOW, YELLOW-ORANGE, ORANGE, RED-ORANGE, RED, RED-VIOLET, VIOLET, BLUE-VIOLET, BLUE, BLUE-GREEN, GREEN, YELLOW-GREEN. Keep the color wheel for use in later lessons.

ENRICHMENT:

Crayon Scraping: *On white construction paper, using any three colors from the color wheel, color heavily with crayon. Make stripes and shapes. After the paper is completely colored, cover the design with a heavy layer of black crayon. Create a design by scraping off areas of the top layer to let the colors show through.*

Color Squeegee: *Use yellow, orange, red, violet, blue, and green food coloring. Place the colors close together in a line of drips at one end of a piece of white, hard-surfaced paper. With a squeegee, pull the colors across the paper.*

From Experimenting with Art *published by Good Year Books. Copyright ©1992 Shirley Kay Wolfersperger and Eloise Carlston.*

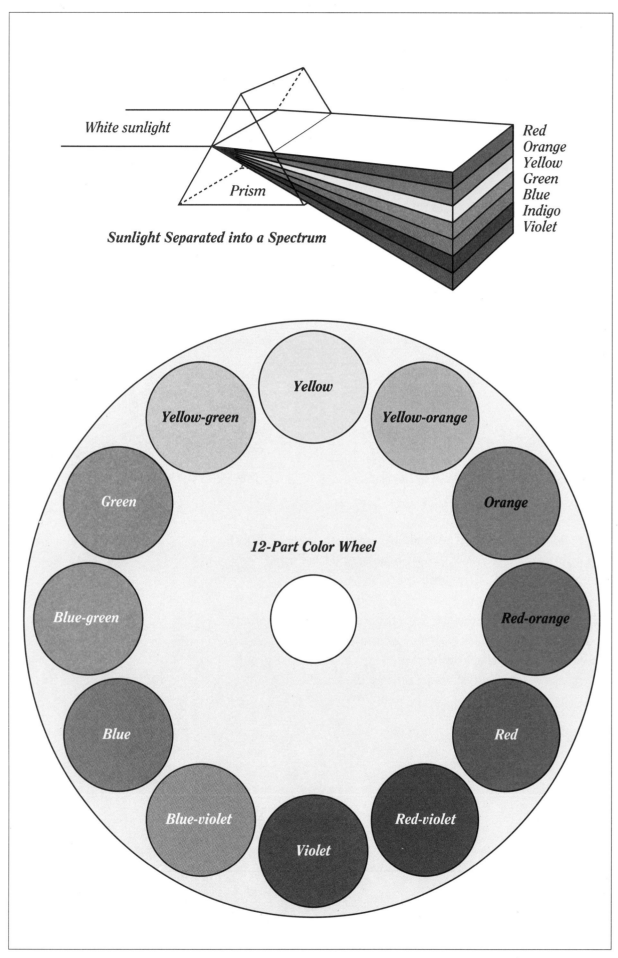

White sunlight

Prism

Sunlight Separated into a Spectrum

Red
Orange
Yellow
Green
Blue
Indigo
Violet

Yellow

Yellow-green

Yellow-orange

Green

Orange

12-Part Color Wheel

Blue-green

Red-orange

Blue

Red

Blue-violet

Red-violet

Violet

CONCEPT TO BE TAUGHT:

In order to study and understand color, we need a special vocabulary. A "hue" is a pure or true color. Red, blue-green, and violet are hues, as are all of the colors we see in the rainbow. All the colors on a twelve-part color wheel are hues.

Colors have values of light and dark. A "tint" is a light value of a hue, and a "shade" is a dark value of a hue. A tint is a hue with white added to lighten it. Pink is a tint of the hue red. Light green is a tint of green, and a peach color is a tint of red-orange. A shade is a hue with black added to darken it. Navy blue is a shade of blue. Maroon is a shade of red, and khaki is a shade of yellow-green. The brown colors are shades of yellow, yellow-orange, or orange.

MATERIALS:

White drawing paper, crayons

EXPERIMENT 1. Find examples in the classroom, including clothing, of hues, tints, and shades.

EXPERIMENT 2. Use Hue, Tint, and Shade Worksheet *(page 73).* Or use crayons on white drawing paper to color and label three examples each: HUES, TINTS, and SHADES.

EXPERIMENT 3. Divide the class into three groups. Have the first group make shape designs with crayons using only hues. Have the second group make shape designs with tints, and the third group make shape designs with shades. Compare the results.

ENRICHMENT:

Initial Mosaic: *Cut construction paper or paint-sample chips of hues, tints, and shades into small pieces. On white paper, using a hue or shade, glue the pieces so they make your initials in "mosaic" letters. Fill in the background using a tint.*

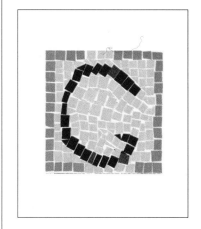

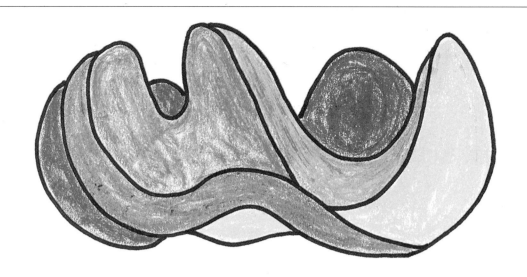

Shape Design with Hues

Shape Design with Tints

Shape Design with Shades

CONCEPT TO BE TAUGHT:

The color wheel is set up in a special way so that we can see how colors are related. "Complements" are two colors that are opposite each other on a color wheel. As you look at the color wheel from Lesson 18, you'll see that red and green are complements. Violet and yellow are also complements, as are red-orange and blue-green.

Complements relate *two* colors on a color wheel, while "triads" relate *three* colors that are farthest away from each other on a color wheel. The primary colors—red, blue, and yellow—form a triad. "Primaries" are basic colors that cannot be achieved by mixing other colors.

Another triad is the secondary colors—orange, violet, and green. "Secondaries" are called that because each one is made by mixing two of the primaries. For instance, red and yellow mixed together make orange; red and blue make violet; and yellow and blue make green.

The "intermediaries" also form triads. The intermediaries are between the primaries and secondaries on the twelve-part color wheel. They are the "two-word" colors, such as yellow-orange, blue-green, and red-violet.

MATERIALS:

White drawing paper, crayons, scissors, color wheels from Lesson 18

EXPERIMENT 1. Use the Complements and Triads Worksheet #1 *(page 74)*. Or on white drawing paper, make pointers for your color wheel using Worksheet #1 as a pattern. On another piece of white paper, color and label the complement for ORANGE. Also color and label the complement for BLUE-VIOLET. Next, color and label the triad with RED in it. Then color and label the triad with BLUE-GREEN in it.

EXPERIMENT 2. Do the Complements and Triads Worksheet #2. *(page 75)*. Or on white drawing paper, draw a shape design and color it using the three colors of an intermediary triad.

ENRICHMENT:

Faraway Flags: *Design a flag for an imaginary country. Use at least one primary and one secondary hue to color it. On the back of the flag, name your "new" country.*

From Experimenting with Art *published by Good Year Books. Copyright ©1992 Shirley Kay Wolfersperger and Eloise Carlston.*

Shape Design with Intermediary Triad Colors
(Barrett, Grade 3)

CONCEPT TO BE TAUGHT:

Artists mix paints in order to obtain the colors they want. With paint in the three primary colors, plus black and white, we can mix most other colors. Mixing red and blue creates violet, mixing blue and yellow makes green, and mixing red and yellow makes orange. Violet, green, and orange, of course, are the secondary colors. Adding white to any of the primary or secondary colors makes a tint. Adding black to these colors makes a shade.

If we mix a color with its complement, such as yellow with violet, we get a "tone" or a grayed color. What we are actually doing when we mix a color with its complement is combining all the primaries. For example, red and blue (both primaries) make violet, which, added to yellow (the third primary), violet's complement, makes a gray.

If a primary color and a secondary color are mixed, we obtain an intermediary color. For instance, if we mix yellow and orange, the result is yellow-orange.

MATERIALS:

Clear glass jars, liquid poster paints: yellow, red, blue, white, black, brushes, heavy paper or cardboard

EXPERIMENT **1.** With clear glass jars, and liquid yellow, red, blue, white, and black poster paints, show the class the primary colors. Mix the secondary colors. Next, mix some examples of tints and shades. Finally, mix two complements to obtain a gray tone.

EXPERIMENT **2.** Use the Color Mixing Worksheet *(page 76)*.

EXPERIMENT **3.** On heavy paper or cardboard, paint a picture using yellow, red, blue, white, and black poster paint. Mix these paints to make any other colors needed.

ENRICHMENT:

Drop Paintings: *Spread newspapers on desks. Dip white paper into a tray of water and place on the newspapers. Drop watercolors onto the wet paper. Let them spread and blend, creating interesting color mixes.*

From Experimenting with Art *published by Good Year Books. Copyright ©1992 Shirley Kay Wolfersperger and Eloise Carlston.*

Color Formulas

Yellow	+	red	=	orange
Yellow	+	blue	=	green
Red	+	blue	=	violet

Yellow	+	orange	=	yellow-orange
Red	+	orange	=	red-orange
Red	+	violet	=	red-violet
Blue	+	violet	=	blue-violet
Blue	+	green	=	blue-green
Yellow	+	green	=	yellow-green

Any hue	+	white	=	a tint

Any hue	+	black	=	a shade

Any hue	+	its complement	=	any hue grayed or softened (tone)

Vermilion red	+	yellow-orange	=	orange hues
Turquoise blue	+	yellow	=	yellow-greens & greens
Purplish red	+	ultramarine blue	=	violets
Orange	+	violet	=	soft red
Green	+	violet	=	soft blue
Orange	+	green	=	dull yellow

Orange	+	black	=	brown
Orange	+	blue	=	brown
Yellow	+ red	+ blue	=	brown
Orange	+ green	+ violet	=	brown

CONCEPT TO BE TAUGHT:

Adjacent colors help us relate similar colors. Both complements and triads relate colors that are far away from each other on the color wheel, but adjacent colors are next to each other. There are three or more colors in adjacent "runs." An example of adjacent colors is the run of red, red-violet, violet, and blue-violet. Adjacent colors also can be all the tints and shades of a color run, such as light blue (a tint), turquoise blue (a hue), dark blue (a shade), and lavender (a tint).

Monochrome color schemes have only one color, while adjacent color runs have at least three colors. "Monochrome" is from two Greek words, *mono* meaning "one" and *chromo* meaning "color." A monochrome scheme includes the hue and all of its shades and tints. For instance, a maroon, red, light red, and pink composition is a monochrome scheme. Any monochrome color scheme may also have black and white in it.

Another type of color scheme is an "achromatic" scheme, which includes only black, white, or grays. In Greek, *a* means "none" and *chromo* means "color," so achromatic means "no-color." A lead pencil drawing is achromatic, as are charcoal drawings and black-and-white photographs.

MATERIALS:

Construction paper, scissors, rubber cement (or paste), color wheels from Lesson 18

EXPERIMENT **1.** Use the Adjacent Colors and Monochromes Worksheet *(page 77)*. Or use the worksheet as a pattern to make a "mask" for locating adjacent colors on the color wheel. Name an adjacent color run with ORANGE in it. Name an adjacent color run with BLUE-GREEN in it.

EXPERIMENT **2.** Use a monochromatic or an achromatic color scheme to make a "stripe" design by gluing down different widths of construction paper. Lines and textures may be added.

ENRICHMENT:

Achromatic Class Collage: *Collect any gluable items, such as yarn, small seashells, paper clips, etc., that are white, black, or gray. Using a large piece of white or black poster board, arrange the items into an achromatic collage.*

Adjacent Figures: *Cut out a figure from a magazine and glue it on oak tag. Cut it out, once again, from the oak tag, making a traceable pattern. Use your color wheel to find three adjacent colors and match them as closely as possible to colored construction paper. With the pattern, trace and cut out one figure from each color. Mount the magazine figure first on a contrasting piece of construction paper. Then mount the three "adjacent" figures following it.*

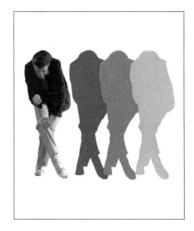

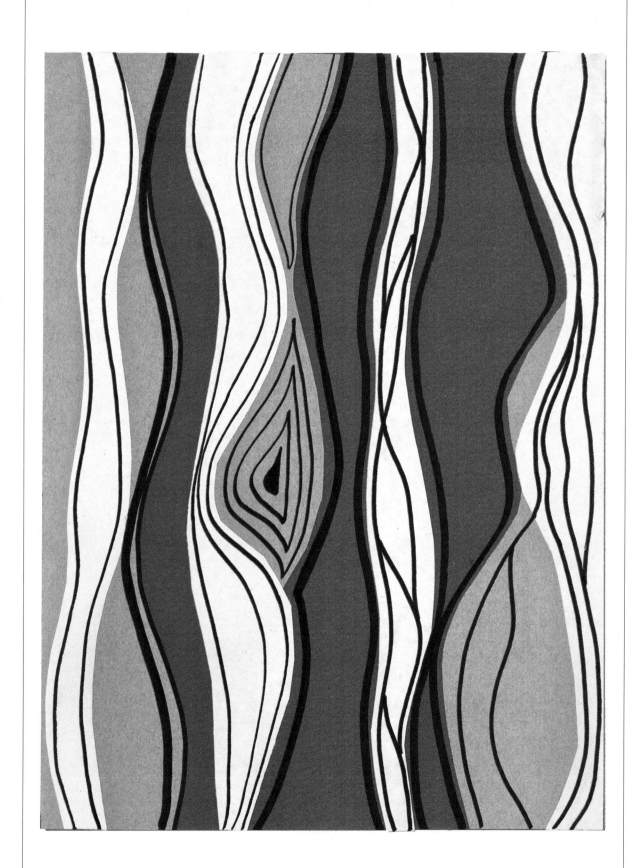

Monochromatic Stripe Design
(Jenny, Grade 5)

CONCEPT TO BE TAUGHT:

Colors are generally divided into warm colors and cool colors. The warmer colors are the sun colors—yellow, orange, and red. The cooler colors are the sea and sky colors—blue, green and violet. Black, which absorbs all color, seems to be warm. White, which reflects all colors, seems to be cool. Warm and cool colors influence how we dress. In the hot summer, we wear cool, light-colored clothes, and in the winter we wear warm, dark-colored clothes.

Colors can also influence our emotions. Warm colors make us feel enthusiastic and energetic. Cool colors make us feel calm and peaceful.

Some cool colors can seem warmer than other cool colors. For instance, violet and green are both cool colors, but violet has more warmth than green. Likewise, some warm colors are cooler than others. Yellow-orange seems cooler than bright red.

Complements are contrasts of warm and cool colors. In complementary color pairs, such as red and green, one of the colors is always warm and one is always cool. Complements intensify and enhance each other when they are together. Red makes green seem greener and cooler, while green makes red seem hotter and brighter.

MATERIALS:

Crayons, colored construction paper, rubber cement (or paste)

EXPERIMENT 1. Use the Warm and Cool Colors Worksheet *(page 78)*. Or discuss warm and cool colors, deciding which color is warmest and which is coolest. Using the color wheel, classify the following eight colors into warm and cool categories: yellow-green, red-orange, blue, violet, orange, green, blue-violet, and red.

EXPERIMENT 2. Give a whole sheet of warm-colored construction paper to half the class, and give cool-colored construction paper to the other half. Give half-sheets of several cool colors to the first group, and half-sheets of several warm colors to the second group. Tear the half-sheets to form shape designs. Glue the designs in place. The first half will have torn-paper designs of cool colors on warm backgrounds, and the second half will have designs of warm colors on cool backgrounds.

ENRICHMENT:

Color Turn-Around: *Make colored marker or watercolor pictures, switching the colors so that the warm colors become cool colors and the cool colors become warm colors. For example, instead of a yellow sun, make a cool-colored sun in a hot sky.*

From Experimenting with Art *published by Good Year Books. Copyright ©1992 Shirley Kay Wolfersperger and Eloise Carlston.*

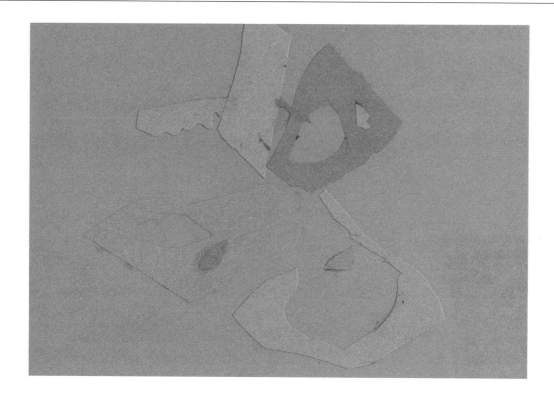

Torn-Paper Design with Cool colors on Warm Background
(Patrick, Grade 1)

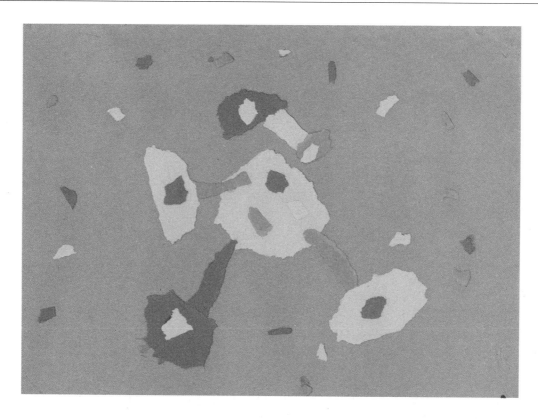

Torn-Paper Design with Warm Colors on Cool Background
(Michelle, Grade 1)

CONCEPT TO BE TAUGHT:

Colors are "relative" because they seem to change depending on other colors that they are near. For instance, if we put an orange square on a blue background, the orange seems brilliant, almost shimmering. If we put the same orange square on a yellow-orange background, it doesn't stand out. The background is actually "robbing" the orange of its intensity and brilliance. Orange and yellow-orange are adjacent colors on the color wheel, and have less contrast, as do other adjacent colors. The highest contrasting colors are yellow and black. Because they are so visible, yellow and black are used for danger signs on highways. The warmth and coolness of a color is relative also. Next to green, red-violet seems very warm. However, placing red-violet next to red makes the red-violet seem cooler. The highest contrast of warmth and coolness between complements is red-orange and blue-green.

Color relates to a country's culture. For instance, when we see the patriotic colors red, white, and blue, we feel an emotional response about the United States, but Mexican citizens must see red, white, and green to feel the same emotional response. Different colors can have the same emotional meaning in separate cultures. A bride in the United States traditionally wears white, but a bride in Japan wears red.

Holidays are often associated with certain colors. Red and green are linked so closely with Christmas that we cannot see them without thinking of Santa Claus and decorated trees. Orange and black have the same association with Halloween witches and pumpkins. In fact, there are very few holidays that don't have a relationship with color.

MATERIALS:

Crayons, magazine pictures, colored construction paper

EXPERIMENT **1.** Use the Relative Color Worksheet *(page 79)*. Discuss.

EXPERIMENT **2.** Cut out a color picture from a magazine. Decide which color of construction paper will make the best frame. Try many different colors. Explain your choices.

ENRICHMENT:

Accordian Pictures: *Using white construction paper, make a fan with one-inch accordian folds. Flatten the paper, and pencil-in a winter scene on every other fold. On the alternate folds, do exactly the same scene as it would appear in the spring. Color with crayons. Refold and mount it. As you walk by, the scene magically changes from winter to spring.*

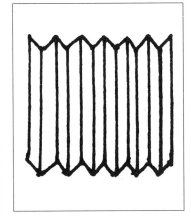

From Experimenting with Art *published by Good Year Books. Copyright ©1992 Shirley Kay Wolfersperger and Eloise Carlston.*

Water Lily and Arrowhead

Color Framing: *Orange is a good choice for the frame because it helps emphasize the vibrant color of the leaves and dragonflies. A brown background would be a good second choice because it would make the whole design stand out. Black and dull green would tend to emphasize the background color too much. What color would you choose for the background frame?*

(From Floral Patterns *by M. P. Verneuil. New York: Dover Publications, 1981)*

CONCEPT TO BE TAUGHT:

Every work of art needs a unifying force. Unity, also known as harmony, pulls together all the elements of design into one pleasing composition. Each part of a design has to relate to other parts of the design. A single theme or idea may unify a design. Another unifying factor is repetition, such as a color that is repeated, a series of lines similarly curved, or a large triangle dominating several smaller triangles. Also, similar textures or materials used to create a design can be unifying. For instance, in a fabric collage, the unifying factor is that all parts of the design are made of fabric. Finally, a related border drawn around a design, or a frame, can be a unifying factor.

EXPERIMENT 1. Use the Unity Worksheet *(page 80)*. Or discuss and review the elements of design and color.

EXPERIMENT 2. Chose several works of art from the Art Source *(page 85)* and discuss their unifying factors.

EXPERIMENT 3. Create a unified design in any medium. Mount and exhibit the design.

FINAL PROJECT SUGGESTIONS:

Latch-Hook Rugs: *Latch-hooking consists of knotting pieces of yarn onto a mesh, creating a shag rug. Each student will need mesh, latch-hooks, and pre-cut yarn. Photocopy a piece of latch-hook mesh eight inches square. On the photocopy draw a simple shape design seven inches square. Color with markers, outlining the shapes with black lines. Place the colored design under the actual mesh, tracing the black outline onto it. Keep the design as a guide. With pre-cut yarn pieces and rug hooks, hook the design.*

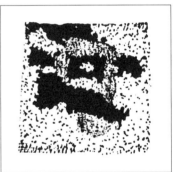

Designer Pillows: *On a seven-inch-square piece of colored burlap or felt, stitch a design with a large blunt needle and several colors of yarn. Use basic embroidery stitches. With a backing piece of burlap, stitch the pillow together with a whip stitch along three sides. Stuff with batting. Stitch the fourth side closed. Make and attach tassels of yarn.*

Horn Poppies

Unifying Factors*: The unifying factors of this design are the repeating shapes in the heads of the flowers, the leaves, and the stems. The bands of color that repeat throughout, the dark brown of the upper background, the poppy heads, the delicate green and off-white of the stems and leaves, and finally, the gray-green band along the bottom, help unify it into a whole. Even the shape of the background, which repeats the flow of the stems, keeps the design a unified whole. Can you think of any other unifying factors? What are some contrasting factors?*

(From Floral Patterns by M. P. Verneuil. New York: Dover Publications, 1981)

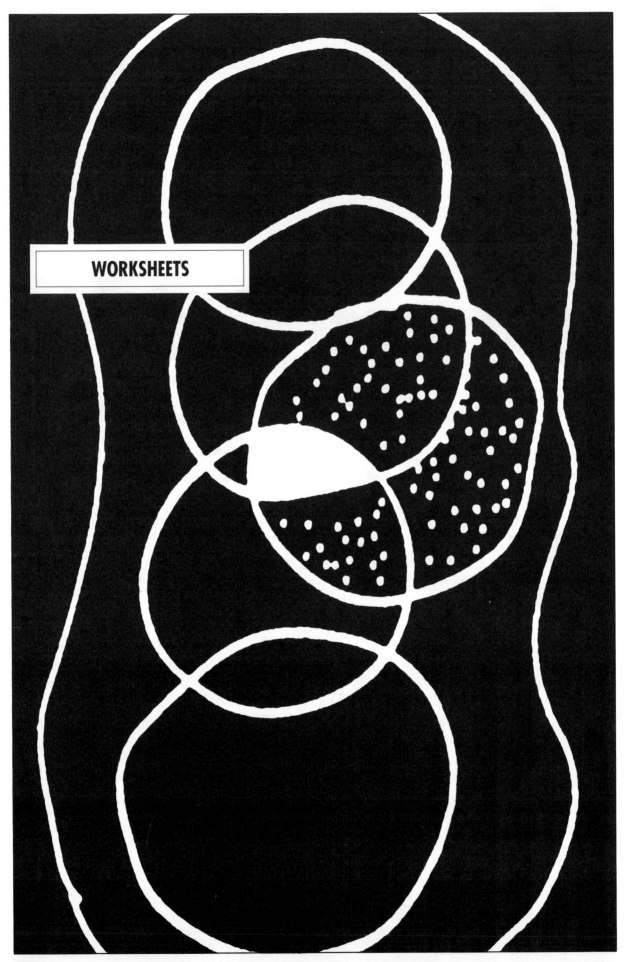

WORKSHEETS

Name _____ Date _____

WORKSHEET: Use a marker to connect the points below with lines, making interesting shapes.

Name .... Date ....

WORKSHEET: Character lines are lines that communicate a mood or feeling by the way they are drawn. Using markers, draw one or two character lines for each mood.

Angry	*Lazy*
Confused	*Happy*

From Experimenting with Art *published by Good Year Books. Copyright ©1992 Shirley Kay Wolfersperger and Eloise Carlston.*

LESSON 3 DIRECTION LINES

WORKSHEET: Direction lines show horizontal, vertical, and diagonal motion in a design. The motion of these lines can be stopped by a line or shape that crosses or tops the line of motion. Using markers, draw *one* or *two* examples of "stop-motion" for each kind of direction line.

Horizontal

Vertical

Diagonal

LESSON 4 **SHAPE**

WORKSHEET #1: Using markers, draw the shapes indicated for each section.

Shapes We Recognize: *such as circles, triangles, and stars.*

Shapes We Don't Recognize: *such as curvy, bumpy, and pointed shapes.*

LESSON 4 **SHAPE**

WORKSHEET #2: ❶ Choose and cut out *five* "stone" shapes of different sizes.
❷ Place the "stones" in an interesting pattern on white paper. Glue them
down. Imagine the stones are in a stream or waterfall. Using a black marker,
draw lines on the paper showing how water would flow around the stones.
Mount the design on black construction paper.

Name _____   Date _____

WORKSHEET: With a marker, outline the contour of each animal.

From Experimenting with Art *published by Good Year Books. Copyright ©1992 Shirley Kay Wolfersperger and Eloise Carlston.*

LESSON 6 **FORM**

WORKSHEET: Use the following words to label each form correctly: Cone, Sphere, Cube, Pyramid, and Cylinder.

Bonus! Name *one* more
three-dimensional shape. ---

LESSON 7 **SIZE**

WORKSHEET #1: Reduce the size of the ice cream sundae by drawing it in the small square.

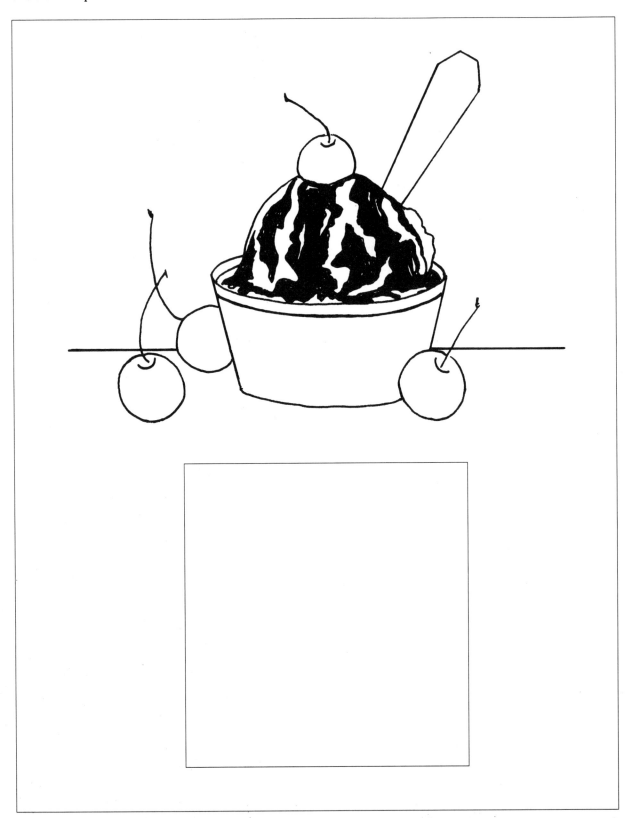

From Experimenting with Art *published by Good Year Books. Copyright ©1992 Shirley Kay Wolfersperger and Eloise Carlston.*

LESSON 7 **SIZE**

WORKSHEET #2: By matching squares, increase the drawing of the turtle to make a "squared enlargement."

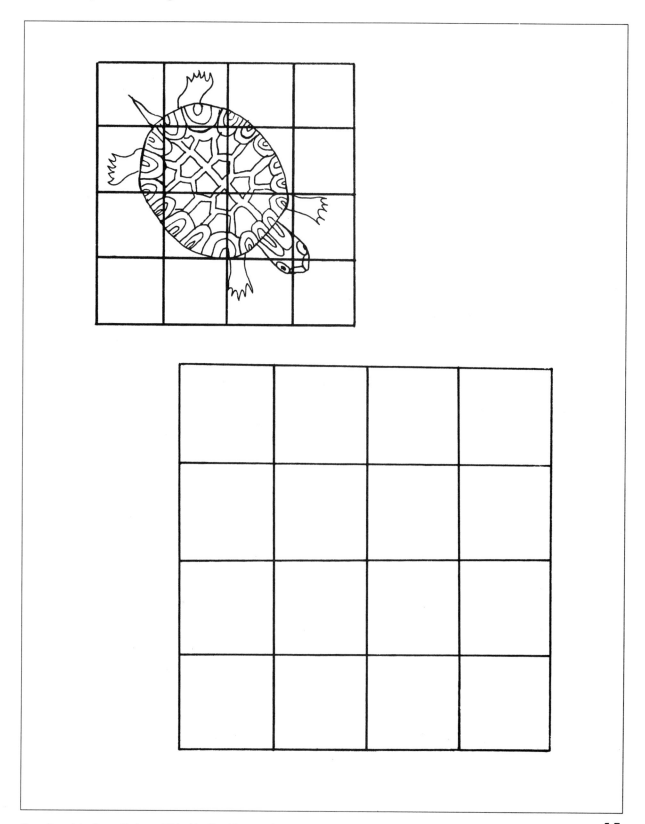

Name _____   Date _____

WORKSHEET: Texture refers to how the surface of something looks and feels. With pencils, draw a texture for each section.

Brick	*Grass*
Fur	*Wood*
Sandpaper	*Hair*
Gravel	*Cloth*

LESSON 9 **REPETITION**

WORKSHEET: With markers, create a design using a shape that you repeat, such as a circle, triangle, or rectangle. You may add points and lines as well.

Name _____   Date _____

WORKSHEET: Most objects in a design are similar. When one object in a design is the opposite or different from others, "contrast" is shown. Using markers, make "contrast" drawings for each section.

Tall and Short	*Circle and Half-Circle*
Light and Dark	*Smooth and Jagged*

From Experimenting with Art *published by Good Year Books. Copyright ©1992 Shirley Kay Wolfersperger and Eloise Carlston.*

LESSON 11 DOMINANCE

WORKSHEET: Making one part of a design *more important* by its size, color, texture, shape, or position in the drawing creates dominance. Make miniature drawings to show dominance by:

Size	*Color*
Texture	*Shape*

LESSON 12   BALANCE

WORKSHEET: Draw an example of balance for each section. Add texture and color to the shapes.

Balance a large shape on one side of the teeter-totter with three or more smaller shapes on the other side.

Put shapes on each side of the teeter-totter so that they are balanced.

  From Experimenting with Art *published by Good Year Books. Copyright ©1992 Shirley Kay Wolfersperger and Eloise Carlston.*

Name _____   Date _____

WORKSHEET: Bilateral symmetry refers to an object or a design that is the same on one side as the other side. Radial symmetry refers to a circular design with a single center. With markers, draw examples for each section.

Bilateral Symmetry

Radial Symmetry

LESSON 14 POSITIVE AND NEGATIVE SPACE

WORKSHEET: ❶ Cut out the L-shaped frames along the heavy black lines. Place the frames around a picture, as shown in the example, making the space larger or smaller as needed. ❷ Use the frames over pictures cut from magazines to show various amounts of negative space. Focus the frames on different parts of the pictures to see what changes take place.

From Experimenting with Art *published by Good Year Books. Copyright ©1992 Shirley Kay Wolfersperger and Eloise Carlston.*

LESSON 15 **COUNTERCHANGE**

WORKSHEET: Color the first half in two colors, one for the foreground and one for the background. Color the second half in the same two colors, but switch them to show counterchange.

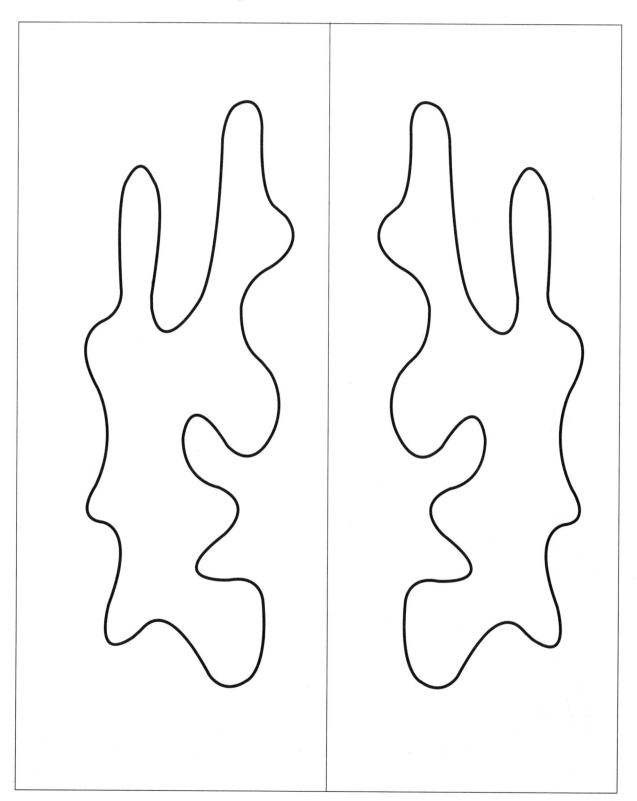

LESSON 16 **VALUE**

WORKSHEET: Using a soft-leaded pencil, match the value of shading or texture in each square of column one with shading or texture in the open squares of column two.

Lightest   *Lightest*

Medium-Light   *Medium-Light*

Medium   *Medium*

Medium-Dark   *Medium-Dark*

Darkest   *Darkest*

From Experimenting with Art *published by Good Year Books. Copyright ©1992 Shirley Kay Wolfersperger and Eloise Carlston.*

LESSON 17 **SIMPLE PERSPECTIVE**

WORKSHEET: Cut out the cactuses in the bottom half and glue them down, putting the large cactuses near the bottom of the scene and the smaller cactuses higher in the picture to show perspective. You may add detail, shadows, and color, if you wish.

Name _____ Date _____

LESSON 18 **COLOR**

WORKSHEET: Use crayons to color the wheel correctly.

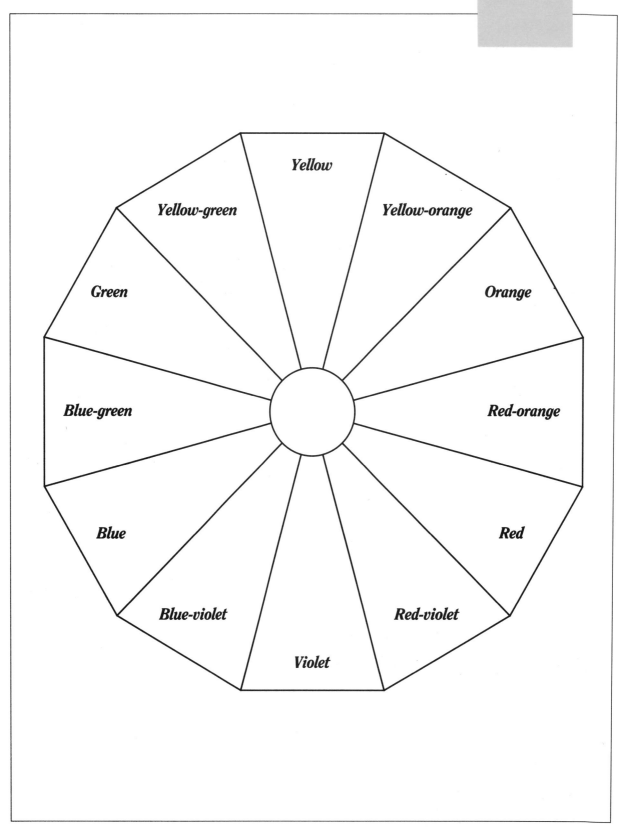

LESSON 19 HUE, TINT, AND SHADE

WORKSHEET: Use crayons to complete the following.

1. Color *three* hues (pure or true colors) and name them.

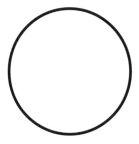 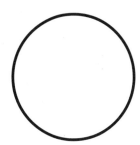 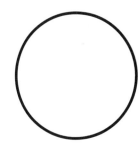

------------------------   ------------------------   ------------------------

2. Color a tint (hue plus white) of:

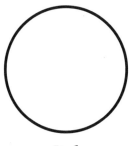 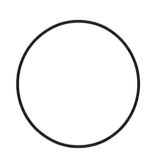 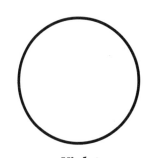

       Red   *Blue*   *Violet*

3. Color a shade (hue plus black) of:

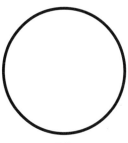 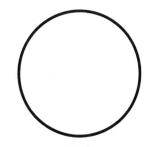 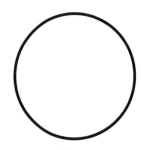

      Blue   *Green*   *Orange*

LESSON 20 COMPLEMENTS AND TRIADS

WORKSHEET #1: ❶ Cut out the pointers at the bottom of this page. Match the circle in the center of each pointer with the circle in the color wheel from Lesson 18 to find complements and triads.   ❷ Use each pointer with the color wheel to complete the following:

1. Complements are opposite colors from each other on a color wheel. Find, color, and label the complement for orange and for blue-violet.

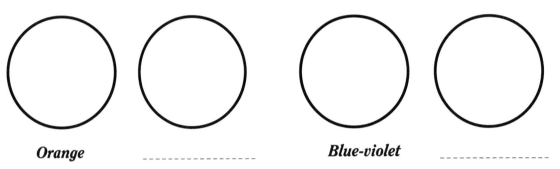

Orange   _ _ _ _ _ _ _ _ _ _   *Blue-violet*   _ _ _ _ _ _ _ _ _ _

2. Triads are three colors that are farthest away from each other on a color wheel. Find, color, and label the triad with red in it and the triad with blue-green in it.

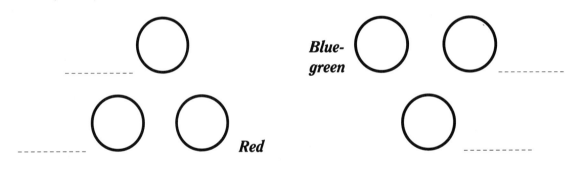

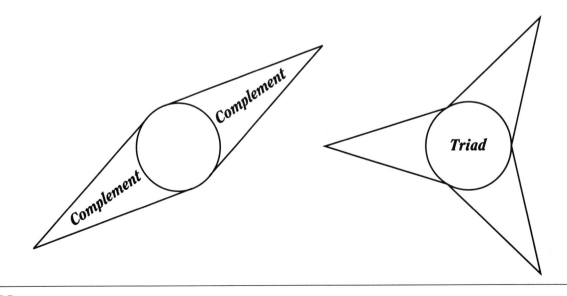

LESSON 20 COMPLEMENTS AND TRIADS

WORKSHEET #2: Intermediary triads are the triads between the primary and secondary triads on a color wheel. They are the "two-word" colors. Color this design using three colors from an intermediary triad.

(From The New Book of Chinese Lattice Designs *by Daniel Sheets Dye. New York: Dover Publications, 1981)*

LESSON 21 **COLOR MIXING**

WORKSHEET: Use yellow, red, and blue poster paint to color the inner circles. Then mix yellow, red, and blue to color the outer circles. Follow the arrows.

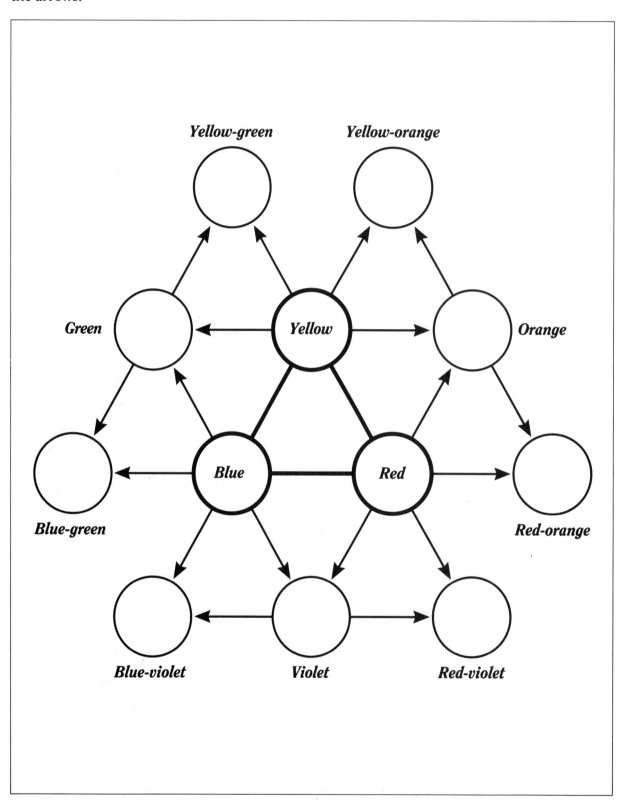

From Experimenting with Art *published by Good Year Books. Copyright ©1992 Shirley Kay Wolfersperger and Eloise Carlston.*

LESSON 22 **ADJACENT COLORS AND MONOCHROMES**

WORKSHEET: Adjacent colors are colors that are next to each other on a color wheel. Three or more adjacent colors in a row on the wheel are said to be in an "adjacent run."

Below is a tool known as a "mask." The mask is connected to a color wheel at the center. It covers all of the colors on the wheel *except* for four, which allows you to see an adjacent run. Cut out the mask and use it to locate adjacent colors on the color wheel. Then answer the questions below.

1. Name an adjacent color "run" that has *orange* in it:

-------------------   -------------------   -------------------   -------------------

2. Name an adjacent color "run" that has *blue-green* in it:

-------------------   -------------------   -------------------   -------------------

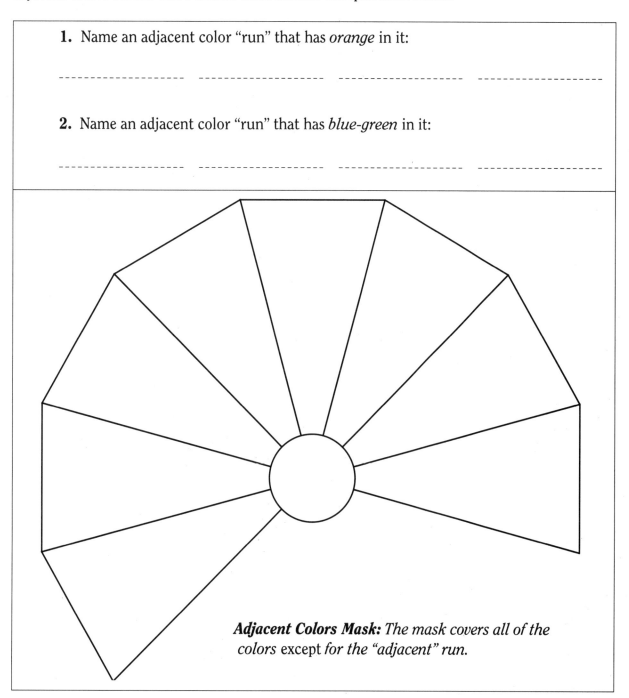

Adjacent Colors Mask: *The mask covers all of the colors except for the "adjacent" run.*

From Experimenting with Art published by Good Year Books. Copyright ©1992 Shirley Kay Wolfersperger and Eloise Carlston.

LESSON 23 WARM AND COOL COLORS

WORKSHEET: Answer each question. Use your color wheel, if needed.

1. What do you feel is the warmest color on your color wheel? ------------------

2. What do you feel is the coolest color on your color wheel ------------------

3. Use crayons to color each circle correctly:

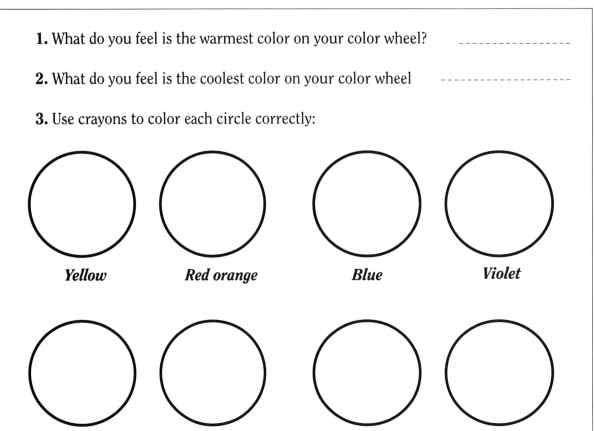

Yellow   *Red orange*   *Blue*   *Violet*

Orange   *Green*   *Blue-violet*   *Red*

4. Using the colors above, put the four warmer colors in the first square and the four cooler colors in the second square.

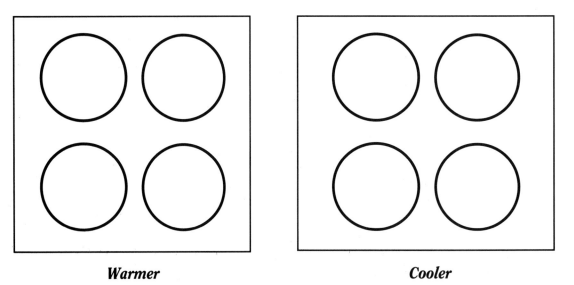

Warmer   *Cooler*

LESSON 24 **RELATIVE COLOR**

WORKSHEET: Colors are "relative" because they seem to change depending on the colors they are near. Color the areas with crayons to see the "relative colors."

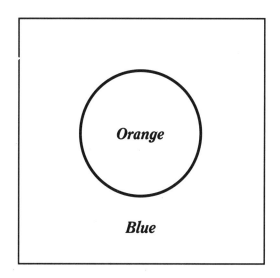

Orange

Blue

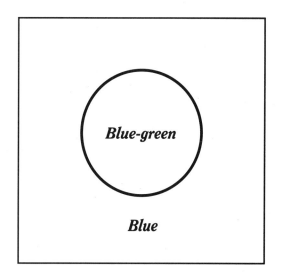

Blue-green

Blue

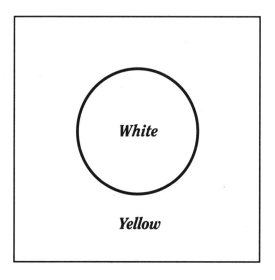

White

Yellow

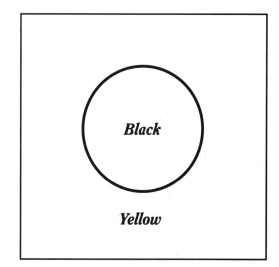

Black

Yellow

Name the colors we associate with:

St. Patrick's Day _____

Valentine's Day _____

Halloween _____

79

LESSON 25 UNITY

WORKSHEET: Draw or write the correct answer for each question.

1. Make a miniature drawing that has *points, lines,* and *shapes* in it.

2. Draw one of each:

Character Line   **Stop-Motion Line**

3. Draw the *contour* of a pencil:

4. Circle the *forms:*

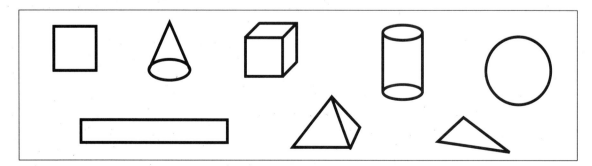

LESSON 25 **UNITY**

5. Make a miniature drawing of rectangles in five different *sizes*.

6. Make a *texture* for this roof.

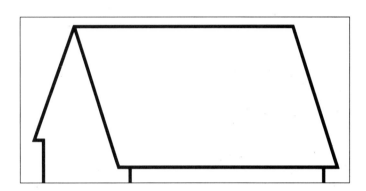

7. Circle the drawing that shows more *repetition* and *rhythm*.

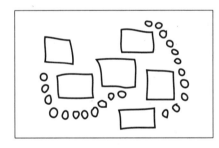 

8. Make a *contrast* drawing of "light and heavy."

LESSON 25 UNITY

9. Circle the *dominant* area of the picture.

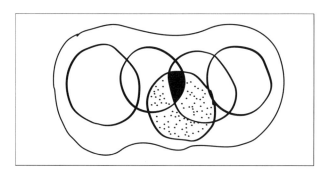

10. *Balance* this drawing.

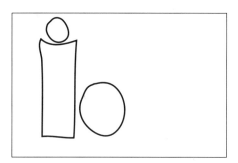

11. Name an example of *bilateral* symmetry. _____

12. Name an example of *radial* symmetry. _____

13. Circle the *positive space* in this drawing.

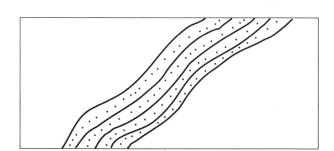

14. Circle the drawing with *counterchange*.

 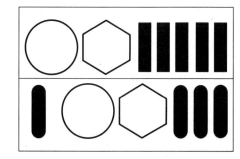

LESSON 25 **UNITY**

15. Circle the rectangle with darker *value*.

16. Make a miniature drawing with *overlapping* shapes.

17. Name and color the three *primary hues*.

- - - - - - - - - - - - - - - -   - - - - - - - - - - - - - - - -   - - - - - - - - - - - - - - - -

18. Name and color the three *secondary hues*.

- - - - - - - - - - - - - - - -   - - - - - - - - - - - - - - - -   - - - - - - - - - - - - - - - -

19. Name and color three *intermediary* colors.

- - - - - - - - - - - - - - - -   - - - - - - - - - - - - - - - -   - - - - - - - - - - - - - - - -

83

LESSON 25 **UNITY**

20. Name a *tint* for red. ---

21. Name a *shade* for blue. ---

22. Name the *complement* of violet. ---

23. Name the *complement* of yellow-green. ---

24. How many colors are in a *triad?* ---

25. Red and yellow mixed together make: ---

26. Yellow and blue mixed together make: ---

27. What color do we add to a hue to make a *tint?* ---

28. What color do we add to a hue to make a *shade?* ---

29. Fill in the word for the missing *adjacent* color: red, -------------------- , violet, blue-violet.

30. *Monochrome* refers to how many colors? ---

31. Name a *warm* color. ---

32. Name a *cool* color. ---

33. What is your favorite color? ---

Art Source

From Experimenting with Art *published by Good Year Books. Copyright ©1992 Shirley Kay Wolfersperger and Eloise Carlston.*

BIBLIOGRAPHY

The Art Institute of Chicago. *Great Impressionist and Post-Impressionist Paintings.* New York: Dover Publications, 1984.

Baumer, Angelica. *Gustav Klimt: Women.* New York: Rizzoli, 1986.

Birren, Faber. *Creative Color.* West Chester, PA: Schiffer Publishing Ltd 1987.

Bristow, Wilanna and Bill. *Color.* Louisville, KY: The Embroiderers' Guild of America, 1978.

Cornia, Ivan E. et al. *Art is Elementary.* Provo, UT: Brigham Young University Press, 1976.

D'Addetta, Joseph. *Traditional Japanese Design Motifs.* New York: Dover Publications. 1984.

D'Addetta, Joseph. *Treasury of Chinese Design Motifs.* New York: Dover Publications, 1981.

Dye, Daniel Sheets. *The New Book of Chinese Lattice Designs.* New York: Dover Publications, 1981.

Dye, Daniel Sheets. *The New Book of Chinese Lattice Designs.* New York: Dover Publications, 1981.

Emerson, Sybil. *Design: A Creative Approach.* Scranton, PA: International Textbook Company, 1957.

Graves, Maitland. *The Art of Color and Design.* New York: McGraw-Hill Book Company, 1941.

Harris, Ann. *Design For Embroidery.* Louisville, KY: The Embroiderers' Guild of America, 1985.

Holme, Bryan. *Enchanted World.* New York: Oxford University Press, 1979.

Itten, Johannes. *The Elements of Color.* New York: Van Nostrand Reinhold Company, 1970.

Jones, Leon. *91 Artists.* Salt Lake City: Utah State Board of Education, 1982.

Mathey, J. F. *Hundertwasser.* New York: Crown Publishers, 1985.

O'Keeffe, Georgia. *Georgia O'Keeffe.* New York: Viking Press, 1976.

Pearson, Ralph M. *The New Art Education.* New York: Harper & Brothers, 1953.

Quin, Gerard. *The Clip Art Book.* New York: Crescent Books, 1990.

Raboff, Ernest. *Art For Children: Albrecht Dürer.* New York: Harper & Row, 1988.

Raboff, Ernest. *Art For Children: Henri Matisse.* New York: Harper & Row, 1988.

Raboff, Ernest. *Art For Children: Pablo Picasso.* New York: Harper & Row, 1982.

Raboff, Ernest. *Art For Children: Raphael.* New York: Harper & Row, 1988.

Scherer, Marge, ed. *Artfully Easy.* New York: Instructor Books, 1983.

Smedley, Delbert W. *Design Principles of Art.* Salt Lake City: Granite School District, 1966.

Utah State Board of Education. *Core Curriculum, 1987, Grades 1-3.* Salt Lake City: Utah State Board of Education, 1987.

Utah State Board of Education. *Core Curriculum, 1987, Grades 4-6.* Salt Lake City: Utah State Board of Education, 1987.

Verneuil, M. P. *Floral Patterns.* New York: Dover Publications, 1981.

Whitney Museum of American Art. *Twentieth-Century Masterpieces from the Whitney Museum of American Art.* New York: Dover Publications, 1988.